The Irish Question

Lawrence J. McCaffrey

The Irish Question

1800-1922

KENTUCKY PAPERBACKS
University of Kentucky Press

to Joan

Preface

In this attempt to present a portrait of the Irish Question, 1800–1922, I am indebted to many scholars of Irish history and literature who have published important books and articles since 1945. I pay tribute to them in the Recommended Reading section, and I hope this book will increase the audience for their significant interpretations of men, movements, and events that have shaped modern Ireland. Much of this book is the product of my own research and writing on Irish nationalism. The Introduction and part of chapter VI first appeared in *Cithara* (I, 3–15) as "The Dimensions of the Irish Question and the Home Rule Crisis, 1910–1914." Chapters I and II contain a small portion of my book, *Daniel O'Connell and the Repeal Year*, published by the University of Kentucky Press in 1966. Chapter IV was first published by the *Review of Politics* (XXII, 72–95) as "Isaac Butt and the Home Rule Movement: A Study in Conservative Nationalism." Much of the material in chapter IV also appeared in my book, *Irish Federalism in the 1870's: A Study in Conservative Nationalism,* published by the American Philosophical Society in 1962. I am indebted to the American Philosophical Society for grants supporting my research in Irish nationalism and to the Research Board of Marquette University for a typing grant.

Contents

Introduction

Frequently historians attribute the origins and successes of Irish nationalism to the failure of the British Government to respond sufficiently or in time to the basic religious, political, economic, and social needs that created and encouraged opposition to the union with Britain. They describe most Government concessions to Irish demands as expedients designed to frustrate agitations before they became insurrections. Because, this argument goes on, these hastily designed sops to Irish claims were palliatives rather than remedies, their deficiencies created new and deepened old grievances, and, in the long run, antagonized rather than conciliated Irish national opinion.

There can be little quarrel with the thesis that Irish nationalism owed much to British ignorance concerning conditions in Ireland and a lack of sympathy and understanding for Irish points of view. Still it is too easy to blame economic exploitation, sectarian strife, and the denial of political expression in Ireland entirely on the inadequacies of British politicians. Even when viewed from a present day perspective the complexity of the Irish Question defied simple solutions, and in their attempt to respond to Irish discontent British leaders were confronted with the limitations placed on political action by the party system, economic and political dogmas, and the pressures and prejudices of British public opinion.

At first glance, the Irish Question appears to have been essentially a religious problem. Protestants, who controlled the Irish Parliament in 1800, accepted the legislative union with Britain as a compact with their coreligionists on the other side of the Irish Sea to maintain the privileged position of Irish Protestantism. Although the Crown and the Tory party endorsed this interpretation of the Act of Union, the Catholic majority in Ireland refused to accept an apartheid policy which doomed it to permanent second class citizenship. But the conflicts which divided Irish Catholic from Irish Protestant involved much more than theological differences.

Through most of the nineteenth century, Protestants, for the most part, were the educated, property owning, prosperous, politically and socially dominant element in Irish society, while Catholics represented the landless, rack-rented, illiterate, and politically underprivileged portion of the community. While most of the emotional content of the Irish Question centered on the religious issue, its essence was the attempt of a besieged minority, aided by an alien legislature, to maintain religious, political, economic, and social ascendancy over a deprived and resentful majority increasingly aware of the power of organized and disciplined numbers. In Ireland, religion symbolized all the interests that distinguished a defensive, parasitic aristocracy from the ambitious and aggressive peasant masses.

Modern Irish nationalism emerged in the nineteenth century as a badge of dignity and a promise of hope for a people who in the century before had lost these human qualities. Nationalism as a mass movement was born in the struggle for Catholic Emancipation and revitalized in the agitations for Repeal, Home Rule, and tenant right. Because the demoralized masses at the beginning of the nineteenth century were indifferent to the bond of nationality, the Act of Union, by providing Catholic representation in the British Parliament, might have frustrated the evolution of nationalism as a vital force in Irish affairs if Britain had used the opportunity to solve Ireland's basic problems. By the 1840's, however, O'Connell's success in mobilizing Catholic opinion for religious and political purposes and Young Ireland's skill in defining and preaching an ideology of cultural nationalism had made the Irish masses conscious of their strength and had convinced them of their superiority over the "materialistic" and "bloodthirsty" Saxons holding them in bondage. The obstinacy of the Protestant Ascendancy in resisting logical and just concessions to the religious, economic, and political needs of the Catholic majority, coupled with the repeated failures of Parliament to cope with these problems, strengthened the "racial" and cultural aspects of the national movement and made a solution of the Irish Question short of self-government impossible.

In general, Liberal Prime Ministers found it less difficult to deal with Irish discontent than their Conservative counterparts. Among the Whig, Liberal, and Radical components of the coalition that made up the Liberal party there was extensive sympathy for such reforms as Catholic Emancipation, an expanded Irish suffrage, a state system of Irish elementary education, and restrictions on the wealth and influence of the Established Church. Nevertheless, in the first half of the nineteenth century, even the Liberals exhibited mental and emotional blocks when confronting the demands of Irish Catholics. Laissez faire doctrines of the classical economists, an important element of the Liberal creed, served the interests of industrial England, but were inapplicable to such Irish problems as landlord-tenant relations, unemployment, overpopulation, and the consequences of these problems, famine. Radicals committed to the secular state obstructed the development of adequate systems of secondary and university education in Ireland because Irishmen were reluctant to accept any plan for education that divorced intellectual training from theological considerations. All factions within the Liberal party, though friendly to various forms of Continental and Latin American nationalism, were cool to Irish claims of sovereignty. They insisted that the Union was essential to Britain's defenses and to the maintenance of the Empire, and they accepted the common Protestant position that Home Rule would be a mask for "Rome Rule".

In the period following 1868, however, Liberals made it increasingly clear that they were willing to go to previously rejected lengths to pacify Ireland. This remarkable change of position resulted from Gladstone's sincere desire to solve the Irish Question, the Liberal party's abandonment of doctrinaire laissez faire for a more flexible approach to economic problems, and Parnell's success in organizing a disciplined, talented, and determined Irish party in the House of Commons. Perhaps more important, Liberal leaders in the late nineteenth century could not ignore the evidence indicating that dynamic Tory imperialism had an attraction for a substantial section of the newly enfranchised working class or the need to compensate for this Conservative advance by enlisting the support of Irish nationalists in the House of Commons. And by 1886, Parnell realized that Home Rule depended on the endorsement of one of the British parties and that the Conservatives would not bid that high for an understanding with the Irish party. Since the Liberals needed the Irish, even at the cost of tenant right and a Parliament in Dublin, and the Irish needed the Liberals, though it meant cooperation with British secularists, Parnell and Gladstone concluded an alliance that weathered many storms and persisted into the First World War.

Conservative politicians were bound by compact, religious

convictions, class privileges, and property interests to the Protestant Ascendancy in Ireland. Irish Protestants depended on the Conservative party to champion their cause in Parliament against the ambitions of the Catholic democracy, and the landed gentry dominating the Conservative party were eager to defend the interests of the Ascendancy. They knew that concessions to the demands of the Catholic masses in Ireland would establish precedents encouraging radical assaults in Britain on the political power and property rights of the aristocracy.

Since the Tories controlled the House of Lords, the Protestant Unionists could destroy legislation tending to curb the privileges of their class or to weaken the connection between Britain and Ireland. When the House of Lords in 1893 made it clear that it would never consent to Home Rule, Irish nationalists finally realized that constitutional methods of agitation would not succeed as long as the peers enjoyed the power to veto Irish independence. Therefore, elimination of the veto power of the House of Lords became a major plank in the Irish party platform. This helped narrow the gap between Irish nationalists, British Radicals, who viewed the Lords as an obstacle preventing the final victory of democracy, and Labour M.P.'s, who considered the peers a barrier to achieving socialism.

Conservative resistance to Irish reform and self-government rested on a strong foundation, the anti-Catholic roots of British nativism. Since the religious conflicts of the sixteenth century, Englishmen had considered Catholicism a menace to British traditions, values, and institutions. The persecution of Protestants by "Bloody" Mary, Spain's use of Catholics as subversives in an effort to destroy Elizabeth, the threat of the Armada, the Catholic issue involved in the struggle between the Stuarts and Parliament, and the seventeenth-, eighteenth-, and early nineteenth-centuries contests with Catholic France all gave Catholicism an alien image in Britain. As late as the early twentieth century, respectable British newspapers and periodicals frightened and excited their readers with "revelations" of Popish plots and Jesuit conspiracies to undermine the Protestant foundations of the British constitution. Since the native Catholic population was timid, quiet, and relatively small, Ireland with her millions of discontended Catholics served as a convenient whipping boy for no-Popery zealots.

After the Act of Union Britons were reluctantly forced to acknowledge the existence of the Irish Question. Irish debates occupied more than a proportionate amount of parliamentary attention to the detriment of vital British and Imperial legislation. Irish agitations—Catholic Emancipation, the tithe war, Father Mathew's temperance movement, the anti-poor law campaign, tenant right, and Repeal—were reported, distorted, and exaggerated in the British press. Curiosity about a geographically close but culturally remote partner in the Union guaranteed interest in Irish writers who described Ireland and the Irish for British readers. Nineteenth-century economic developments also encouraged Irish-British contacts. Every year substantial numbers of Irish peasants supplemented meager incomes by working the British harvest, and the employment possibilities in British factories attracted permanent Irish settlers to the boom towns of England and Scotland.

The information about Ireland and her people that the British gained from reading and personal association did not encourage respect. They were shocked to learn that contempt for British law and order seemed to be part of the Irish national character, and their Protestant, nativist sensibilities were offended by the militant Catholic and anti-unionist views of popular Irish leaders. Britain's industrial and agrarian proletariat resented cheap Irish competition on the labor market. All levels of British society rejected Irish immigrants who spoke English in a strange if melodious manner, demonstrated prodigality in financial matters, drank to excess and engaged in drunken brawls, increased the number of prostitutes walking the streets, worshipped God in a "superstitious" and "idolatrous" manner, and were overly submissive to their clergy, who were servants of the Pope.

Because they were aware of British hostility and were lonely and uncomfortable in an urban environment, these transplanted Irish peasants clung together in their slum ghettoes for mutual comfort and security. By clinging to one another they accented their national vices and peculiarities. British critics of the Irish seldom tried to understand the psychological or sociological reasons for Irish delinquency and clannishness. Instead, they preferred to bolster their egos by attributing Irish behavior patterns to a basic inferiority of character and the malignant nature of Popery. In fact, the Irish played a role in British history from 1800–1922 similar to that of the Negro in American history. They had a useful economic function doing the menial work other people were too weak or too proud to do; they entertained (the happy, shiftless stage Irishman with the rich and comic brogue was a stereotype); they frightened (they were brutal, wild, lawless, uncivilized); and they were convenient targets for the release of inferiority complexes and sadistic tendencies. In response to social and economic conditions, their own weaknesses, and British attitudes, many Irishmen cultivated the character designed for them by the British majority.

British anti-Irish and anti-Catholic opinion, made more formidable by each expansion of the electorate, was a significant emotional factor in British politics, making it difficult for Parliament to approach Irish issues objectively. In the 1840's Sir Robert Peel, as part of his Irish policy, attempted to detach the Catholic hierarchy and clergy from the ranks of Irish nationalism by easing the financial burdens of their church. His efforts antagonized British opinion and the ultra-Tory wing of the Conservative party, which had never forgiven him for conceding Catholic Emancipation in 1829. In revenge for Peel's endowment of the Roman Catholic seminary at Maynooth and his work in repealing the Corn Laws, the ultra-Tories combined with the Whigs to turn the leader of their party out of office. The price of vengeance was a seriously weakened Conservative party and the political confusion and instability of the 1850's and 1860's.

No-Popery British nativism continued to influence the course of British politics in the last half of the nineteenth and the early decades of the twentieth centuries. Gladstone too discovered that British opinion could respond unfavorably to Government efforts to satisfy the needs and the demands of Irish opinion. Like Peel, he split his party in an attempt to solve the Irish Question. With the completion of the Irish-Liberal alliance, followed by a split in the Liberal party over Home Rule, the anti-Catholic, anti-Irish orientation of British opinion became the most powerful weapon in the Conservative, renamed Unionist, party arsenal and the Irish alliance the most vulnerable chink in the Liberal armour.

The attempts of Peel and Gladstone to reconcile Irish aspirations with British domestic and imperial interests, in the face of hostile British opinion and dissent within their own parties, produced some of the most dramatic episodes in nineteenth-century British history. However, the most illuminating example of the influence of the Irish Question on British politics, and the difficulty of solving this question in atmosphere dominated by no-Popery sentiment, occurred in the period 1910–1914, when the crisis over Home Rule drove Britain to the precipice of civil war.

By 1910 the old grievances over land, religion, voting, and education had, for the most part, been laid to rest by reforming Liberal and Unionist administrations. But Irish nationalism survived and took on an existence independent of all the economic, social, political, and religious issues that had created and nourished it. In 1910 and 1911 Irish nationalists played the leading role in the dramatic defeat of their old enemy, the House of Lords. When the third Home Rule bill came before Parliament in 1912, it brought about a direct confrontation between Irish nationalists and the British Tories allied with Protestant Ireland. No bribes were available to British politicians to divert the attention of Irish nationalism, and no constitutional barriers remained to frustrate its victory. Since the Unionists had lost the Constitutional game, they decided to encourage armed rebellion against Parliament by the Protestants of northern Ireland. By August 1914 Britain faced the prospect of civil war. She was rescued from the grim dilemmas of the Irish Question by World War I. When the slaughter on the Continent was over, a weary Britain faced a new generation of Irish nationalists disillusioned with British politics and British constitutionalism. These young men placed their confidence in the bullet and the grenade.

CHAPTER ONE

Catholic Emancipation, 1800-1829

In the 1790's Britain was engaged in a life and death struggle with the armies of the French Revolution. The citizen soldiers of France, with their high morale, were winning decisive victories against Britain's Continental allies. British leaders feared that France would try to invade the British Isles and that Ireland, with her class and religious conflicts, was a natural target for French ambitions. If Ireland was invaded and occupied by France, Britain would be trapped between an Ireland and a Western Europe dominated by her old enemy and the spirit of revolution.

The fears of British politicians concerning the future of Ireland were shared by many members of the Irish Protestant aristocracy and gentry. They were convinced that Ireland was in danger from two forces: French inspired democracy and an aggressive Catholicism emerging from the degradation of the Penal Law period. The unsuccessful but destructive French-supported Irish rebellion of 1798, which brought together the radical middle-class United Irishmen and the peasantry (Catholics from the South and Protestants from the North) in an effort to establish a democratic republic, seemed to confirm the anxieties of the Establishment.

William Pitt the Younger, the British Prime Minister, and his Cabinet were convinced that the Irish Parliament lacked the public confidence and the funds to insure the tranquility of Ireland or her independence from French influences. They approached Protestant leaders with an offer of Union with Britain. Although many members of the Protestant Ascendancy were attracted by the offer, believing that the Union would prove economically beneficial to Ireland and at the same time guarantee their privileged position against the threats of Jacobinism and Romanism, a majority of Protestant leaders were hostile to the Union. They felt that the British Parliament might make concessions to Catholic agitation and that the transfer of power to Westminister would diminish the political influence of the Irish aristocracy and threaten Irish economic interests. British officials won substantial support for the Union from Catholic religious and lay leaders by suggesting to them, with the approval of Pitt, who favored Catholic Emancipation, that a British Parliament would deal more objectively with Catholic claims than the Dublin Parliament dominated by the Protestant Ascendancy. There were also Catholic patriots who preferred to place their confidence in an Irish Protestant Parliament rather than in a Protestant British legislature.

In 1799 the Irish Parliament rejected the Union, but by 1800 the British Government had made a few converts from among the anti-Unionist ranks and had persuaded a large number of neutrals to join the Unionist cause. In that year a majority of the M.P.'s in the exclusively Protestant Irish Parliament voted the extinction of their country's independence. Traditional interpretations of the Act of Union have attacked the British Government for using patronage positions and peerages to bribe members of the Irish Parliament to vote for the Union. A recent study, G. C. Bolton's *The Passing of the Irish Act of Union* (London, 1966), ably argues that the charges of corruption have been exaggerated. The use of patronage to win votes was an accepted practice in eighteenth-century Ireland, one employed by all factions.

Bolton insists that those who voted for the Union did so for a wide variety of reasons, as did those who voted against it. Motives in both cases were sometimes disinterested and thoughtful, sometimes selfish and mercenary.

In 1800, then, leaders of the Protestant community in Ireland traded their country's sovereignty for the protection of their privileged position in the Irish community, 100 seats in the British House of Commons and thirty-two places in the House of Lords (four bishops and twenty-eight lay peers), the union of their Church with the English Church in the United Church of England and Ireland, and the amalgamation of the Irish and British treasuries (completed in 1817). But the union between Britain and Ireland was not as complete as the union between England and Scotland in 1707. Ireland retained a separate Executive comprised of a Lord Lieutenant and a Chief Secretary and his staff, courts, police, prisons, and a number of agencies and departments of government. Ireland had an ambiguous position in relation to Britain: it was half integrated into the British system, half a colonial dependency. On August 2, 1800, the Irish Parliament in College Green held its last session. About five months later, on January 28, 1801, the Irish representatives took their places in the Parliament of the United Kingdom of Great Britain and Ireland. Thus began the history of the Irish Question in British politics—the most difficult, the most persistent, the most emotional, and perhaps the most significant problem to confront British politicians in the period 1800–1922.

The Union was not responsible for the social, religious, economic, or even all of the political dimensions of the Irish Question, but it complicated an already difficult situation. Religious differences were the most obvious areas of tension in Irish society. Well over 75 percent of the Irish population were Roman Catholics. Although a large majority, they were taxed to support the established Protestant church which ministered to the spiritual needs of only about 13 percent of the people (Presbyterians, Methodists, Quakers and other Nonconformists also paid tithes). The Protestant minority not only enjoyed a favored religious position, but also owned most of the property in the country and had a monopoly on seats in Parliament and Government office.

Protestant Ascendancy had been legalized by the Penal Laws enacted by the Irish Parliament in the late seventeenth and early eighteenth centuries, following the failure of James II and his Irish Catholic and French allies to reverse the Glorious Revolution of 1688. Irish Catholic soldiers fought better than the Stuarts deserved and negotiated honorable terms in the Treaty of Limerick (1691). They were permitted to join the armies of the Bourbons and the Hapsburgs on the Continent. Their relatives who remained in Ireland were promised religious toleration and respect for their property rights, but the Irish Protestant Parliament refused to honor the commitment made by William III and took advantage of the exile of the Catholic gentry to impose a harsh settlement on Papists.

Scholars present different interpretations of the ultimate objectives of the Penal Laws. Perhaps they were intended as an effort to demoralize Catholics, and thus destroy them as a revolutionary danger; or as a program to make life so uncomfortable for Catholics that they would embrace Protestantism; or as an attack on the property and the status of those members of the Catholic gentry who still remained in Ireland. Whatever the goal, the Catholic peasant masses were terrorized and dehumanized, and the position of the Catholic gentry was diminished and their property threatened. Yet comparatively few Catholics crossed the border from the persecuted state of Popery to the security of Protestantism.

The Penal Laws were many and covered a variety of situations. They restricted the activities of Irish priests, outlawed the hierarchy and religious orders, gave Protestants exclusive control over Irish education, made it difficult for Catholics to own property and easy for Protestants to confiscate Catholic property, and denied Catholics all opportunities to participate in the political life of their country. Papists could not vote, hold Government office or seats in Parliament, or accept commissions in the armed forces.

As the religious bitterness and fanaticism of the sixteenth and seventeenth centuries faded with the increasing sense of security in the Protestant community and the tolerant influences of the Enlightenment, the Penal Laws were mitigated both by nonenforcement and repeal. The Catholic gentry held on to some of its property through the connivance of friendly Protestant neighbors, and the anticlerical laws were often winked at by the authorities. With the menace of the French Revolution and its possible attraction for the persecuted Irish Catholics, the British Government put pressure on the Irish Parliament to make some concessions to the feelings of the Catholic majority. In the 1790's the Irish Parliament gave the franchise to the forty-shilling Catholic freeholders, permitted Catholics to hold commissions in the army under the rank of colonel, and established a Roman Catholic seminary at Maynooth, County Kildare.[1] These concessions meant that Catholics in Ireland enjoyed more privileges than members of the small Catholic minority in Britain.

When Ireland became part of the United Kingdom she had a small Catholic gentry class and an expanding Catholic middle class. This middle class was the product of the early Penal period when Catholics had to turn their energies and ambitions to commerce and the lower ranks of the professions. Although the position of the Catholic gentry and

[1] The forty-shilling freehold vote actually increased the political influence of the Protestant landlords. Without a secret ballot, the Catholic voter could not take an independent position without risking eviction from his farm or loss of employment if he lived in a borough.

middle class had substantially improved in the course of the eighteenth century, they were still frustrated by the remaining Penal Laws, which denied them a significant role in the direction of Irish affairs. They agitated for Catholic Emancipation so they could sit in the House of Commons and the House of Lords, hold Government office, advance in the professions, and win social prestige in the Irish community. In their agitation for Catholic political rights, they had little contact with the Catholic peasant masses.

Most Irish Catholics were tenant farmers, squatters, or agricultural laborers. As a group they were dehumanized, demoralized, and illiterate, possessing neither the hope of progress nor the desire for improvement. Few tenant farmers had farms larger than fifteen acres. The agricultural laborers and the squatters were fortunate to have the use of an acre to provide food for their large families. Most Irish peasants lived in crowded mud huts with dirt floors that turned into mires in the heavy Irish rains. Vermin-filled thatch roofs covered their heads. Often there was not even one window to let in fresh air. Since a pig was often the only valuable family possession, it was kept in the cabin in bad weather. Naturally these living conditions resulted in disease and an extremely high mortality rate. If a person defied his environment and survived childhood, scurvy, cholera, tuberculosis, and hunger would probably cut him down before middle age. Despite the prevalence of disease and famine, and the lack of medical care, Ireland had a population explosion which began midway through the eighteenth century and lasted until the Great Famine of the 1840's. In 1781 the estimated Irish population was 4,048,000; in 1841 the census recorded it at 8,175,000: an increase of about 100 percent in sixty years.

This population explosion that managed to overcome infant mortality, famines, plagues, and filth was the result of early marriages. Poverty seems to encourage the sexual urge, and with pious Irish Catholics desire was satisfied in marriage. And to people as poor and as miserable as the Irish peasant, sex and the companionship of wives and children, like good and even bad whiskey, were a comfort and an escape. But the most important reason for early marriages and the consequent high fecundity of Irish women was the potato. The potato is a vegetable that is easy to cultivate, flourishes in bad soil, and makes a nutritious meal. In the period before the Great Famine, most Irish peasants ate only potatoes and drank a little milk to wash them down. The average Irishman ate ten pounds of potatoes a day; sometimes he consumed them half cooked so they would take longer to digest. The exclusive use of the potato as a source of food made it possible for a family to feed many children on a small piece of land and encouraged people to marry young and raise large families. But the reliance on the potato meant frequent famines. The period 1845–1851 was not the first time that the potato crop was ruined by fungus or bad weather.

The population explosion put too much strain on the already weak agrarian economy. Since there was no industry in Ireland to absorb the surplus population, tenant farmers subdivided their small plots to accomodate a growing population and to earn a few shillings and pence in rent. As Irish farms decreased in size, Irish agriculture increased in inefficiency. Exploiting a shortage of land, landlords were able to raise rents far beyond the value of the land, and they could always find desperate people willing to pay. The tenant paying an inflated rent was anxious to sublease and charge his tenant an excess tribute so that he could meet his obligations to the landlord. Land hunger and the exploitation of this hunger fostered avarice, evictions, class war, and violence. Since the landlords had the support of the law and the authorities, a number of secret societies like the Ribbonmen and the Whiteboys flourished in Ireland.

They burned hayricks and maimed cattle to punish landlords and those who occupied the farms of men evicted for non-payment of rent, they shot bailiffs who represented rack-renting landlords, and they even took action against some Catholic priests who acquired the reputation of charging excessive dues and fees in exchange for their religious services.

A considerable number of Irish landlords were absentees. They lived in Britain. Absenteeism aggravated the social and economic problems associated with the Irish Question. Resident landlords were more likely to be interested in the quality of agriculture practiced on their estates. They might work at improving the agricultural techniques of their tenants and show a humane interest in their welfare. Agents of absentee landlords were often quick to evict and were likely to pay more attention to the collection of rents than to increasing the productivity of the estate. Of course it is difficult to prove that absentees were not as kind or as humane as resident landlords, but they did deny to Ireland the income they derived from their estates, thus frustrating the development of domestic trades and industries. Non-resident proprietors were more British than Irish in points of view, and the loss of such a large proportion of the aristocracy retarded the development of a vital, intelligent, and influential Irish political and economic opinion.

Relations between landlords and tenants were more cordial in Ulster than in Leinster, Munster, and Connacht. Custom in Ulster permitted a tenant to sell his interest in the farm when he left it and protected him against eviction and an unfair raise in rent. But in the South and West, if a tenant improved his farm by draining, fencing, or fertilizing his land or by repairing his buildings he increased the value of the farm, and the landlord might raise his rent. If he could not meet his new obligations he was evicted, without compensation for the improvements he had made. As a result, tenant farmers in Leinster, Munster, and Connacht seldom improved their farms, and the quality of agriculture in Ulster was much higher than in the rest of the country. Perhaps landlord-tenant relations in Ulster were more harmonious because many tenant farmers were Protestants or Nonconformists like their landlords, and religious differences did not intensify class conflict.

All intelligent observers recognized the sick condition of the Irish economy, but the political situation, religious divisions, and the economic dogmas of classical Liberalism obstructed efforts to remedy the situation. Both Whig and Tory politicians refused to consider limitations on property rights. They argued that the agrarian question in Ireland was a moral problem beyond a political solution. Laissez-faire dogmatism, so important in Whig and Radical circles, opposed government programs which included public works and emigration projects, though Whigs and Radicals were willing to give the Irish a greater share in shaping their destiny through political reforms and were sympathetic to the demands for equality between the Catholic and Protestant churches. Some of the Radicals were even prepared to consider alterations in the economic and social structure in Ireland. But the Tories were adamant in opposing any concessions that might diminish Protestant Ascendancy in Ireland. They considered criticisms of the privileged position of the Protestant Church and the Protestant aristocracy an assault on property rights. Catholic Emancipation would encourage Irish agitation and nationalism and open the door to further demands for reform. Radical victories in Ireland would endanger the Union and inspire dangerous agitation against the status quo in Britain.

Before Irish Catholic leaders from the gentry and middle class could transform Whig and Radical good intentions into a specific and dynamic Irish policy and overcome the obstinancy of Tories, they would have to mobilize the

Catholic masses behind their demands for justice. But this seemed an impossible task. The peasant masses, oppressed by political and economic systems, were poor materials for a successful agitation. Catholic Ireland needed a leader possessing the genius to lift the spirits of her beaten and miserable people and give them the hope and confidence necessary for effective political action. In Daniel O'Connell Ireland found such a leader. The Irish Catholic national opinion he created caused British politicians to face the unpleasant alternatives of concession to Irish demands or the risk of revolution, a revolution that would endanger not only the Union but the political, social, and economic status quo in Britain.

Daniel O'Connell created modern Irish nationalism. No Irish politician has had as much international significance. He dedicated his talents and his energy to the interests of Ireland, but the principles he represented, the objectives of his ambitions, and the methods of his agitations had consequences for democratic and liberal causes in every country within the framework of Western Civilization or in contact with it. In the aristocratic and ultraconservative age of Metternich, he was a successful Tribune of the people. O'Connell translated democratic theory into successful practice by molding millions of illiterate Irish peasants into an organized and articulate national opinion. And using this national opinion, he forced a powerful, aristocratic British Government to make concessions to the demands of the Irish masses. In the early nineteenth century O'Connell was one of the most discussed personalities in Europe: to the embattled left, he was a symbol of hope and a promise of the future; to the nervous aristocracy on the right, he represented the enemy attempting to tear down the walls of entrenched privilege.

Of course, O'Connell was most despised by the British Establishment. Their newspapers and periodicals described him as a mendacious, avaricious vulgarian agitating the Irish masses in order to collect money from ignorant and impoverished peasants. Conservative journalists and politicians told the British public that O'Connell was the leader of a vast conspiracy dedicated to subverting the British Empire and the British Constitution by separating Ireland from Britain and by imposing Popery on the British Isles. Since No-Popery was the basic ingredient in British nativism, O'Connell was a natural target for British Tories, who manipulated Protestant passions to maintain the status quo at home and British rule in Ireland.[2]

With O'Connell's entry into politics, the Irish Question became the leading emotional issue dividing British parties and British public opinion. He gave lessons to British politicians in the techniques of political organization and agitation. His successors in the leadership of Irish nationalism continued the instruction.

Born on August 6, 1775, O'Connell in British terms was a member of the Irish Catholic gentry, but to Irishmen he was a Kerry clan chieftain. His father was Morgan O'Connell, but he was adopted by his uncle Maurice, head of the family. Maurice, through the friendship of Protestant neighbors, had managed to keep his property during the penal period and had substantially increased the family wealth in successful smuggling operations. Some of the O'Connells

    [2] O'Connell's impact on Continental and British opinion has been discussed by Terence de Vere White, "English Opinion," and John Hennig, "Continental Opinion" in *Daniel O'Connell,* edited by Michael Tierney (Dublin, 1949). While working on the Repeal agitation of 1843, I read a letter to Lord John Russell from his brother who was traveling in Eastern Europe in 1843. In this letter William Russell said that O'Connell was the talk of Eastern Europe, even among the peasant class. He was viewed as the tribune of his people, the symbol of democracy. (Lord William Russell to Lord John Russell, July 10, 1843, Russell Papers Public Records Office, London). A useful study could be made of the influence of O'Connell on the style and tactics of Irish-American politics and Irish-American political leaders. In general I would argue that the character of Irish-American politics, derived as much from the Irish background as from the American environment.

had earned military reputations in the service of the Bourbons and Hapsburgs. Because the Penal Laws prevented a Catholic education in Ireland, Maurice sent his nephew to France and Belgium for his secondary schooling. The French Revolution forced Daniel to finish his studies in England, where he trained for the bar at Lincoln's Inn. The influence of conservative clerical teachers on the Continent and his experience with the violence of the French Revolution made him a permanent opponent of the use of physical force for political change. His antagonism toward revolution, however, did not create a mental block against Liberalism. He read the philosophes of the Enlightenment and for a time rejected the tenets of orthodox Christianity. In time he regained his faith, but retained the liberal political attitudes of the Enlightenment. While in England O'Connell became a Utilitarian and he always considered himself a friend and loyal disciple of Jeremy Bentham.[3]

O'Connell returned to Ireland to practice law, and in 1802 he married his cousin Mary O'Connell of Tralee. Uncle Maurice disapproved of what he considered an improvident match, but Mary O'Connell was a talented woman who proved an asset to Daniel's political career. Seven children born of the marriage—four sons and three daughters —reached adulthood. Mary O'Connell provided her husband with a great deal of love, wise political advice, and the peace and security of a happy home.

Since the Penal Laws denied them the opportunity for Government office, the law was a difficult profession for

[3] Jeremy Bentham (1748-1832) was trained as a barrister, but concentrated his intellectual efforts on physical science, jurisprudence, ethics, and politics. He was the father of Utilitarianism, which emphasized that the purpose of government was to insure the greatest good for the greatest number. This could be achieved if institutions and laws were rationalized and humanized to encourage a high social ethic. Bentham advocated political democracy and economic laissez faire as the end results of rational government. But Bentham's view of law and government were used by Liberals in the late nineteenth and early twentieth centuries to justify the welfare state.

Catholics. They had to be content with unimportant cases and small fees. But O'Connell worked hard and used his knowledge of the Irish as well as his quick mind, wit, and oratorical skill to become the best cross-examiner and persuader of juries in Ireland. Fees for defending Irish Catholics were small, but his practice was large. By 1828 he was earning between 6,000 and 7,000 pounds a year.

O'Connell used the courtroom to promote his political ambitions. Often in addressing juries he attacked British rule in Ireland and advocated Catholic Emancipation. When O'Connell entered Irish politics, Catholic Emancipation was the prominent issue. Leadership of the Emancipation cause was in the hands of the Catholic nobility and gentry with the support of the equally moderate middle class. In Parliament, Henry Grattan, whose agitation in the 1780's had extended the powers of the Irish Parliament and who had led the Irish parliamentary opposition to the Union, commanded the forces promoting the Catholic cause. Emancipation enlisted the support of most Whig and a few Tory M.P.'s, and on occasion could even command a parliamentary majority. But the Tory Government defied Irish Catholic and parliamentary opinion and could rely on the assistance of the King's Protestant conscience and the militancy of British no-Propery opinion. Emancipation did have one chance of success: a compromise involving the independence of the Catholic Church in Britain and Ireland. Tory leaders indicated a willingness to repeal political restrictions on Catholics in exchange for a veto over the bishops appointed by the Vatican. The veto was acceptable to most of the Catholic leaders in Britain and Ireland, some of the Irish Catholic bishops, Grattan and the British Whigs, and even the Pope, since Rome was anxious to establish friendly relations with the British Government.

O'Connell joined the minority anti-veto section of the Catholic Emancipation movement. He argued that Government intervention in the affairs of the Catholic Church would be detrimental to the interests of religion. His opposition to the veto was consistent with his Benthamite commitment to the separation of church and state, but O'Connell's main motive in fighting an agreement between Britain and the Vatican was his interest in Irish liberty. He realized that the issue of Catholic Emancipation could be exploited to arouse the Irish Catholic masses and turn them into a force for Irish independence. The Church and her bishops and priests were potential instruments of national unity. Most members of the hierarchy and clergy came from the peasant class, and they enjoyed the confidence and respect of the people. As a group they had not participated in politics, but their position in the agrarian society made them natural leaders of the masses. If the British Government was able to secure control over the nomination of bishops, the hierarchy could be used as an instrument of British power. It would be difficult, if not impossible, to organize an effective national movement if the prelates were neutral or hostile to the cause. Therefore, O'Connell reasoned, it would be better to postpone Catholic Emancipation if Emancipation meant the sacrifice of the most important institution in Ireland to British control. O'Connell succeeded in rallying a considerable portion of clerical opinion against the veto. His efforts delayed Catholic Emancipation, but they pushed the bishops and priests down the road of Irish nationalism.

The conflict over the veto split the Catholic ranks, and from 1813 to 1823 the cause drifted. In 1823 O'Connell, Thomas Wyse, and one of the leaders of the vetoist wing, Richard Lalor Sheil, met at the home of O'Connell's son-in-law in the Wicklow mountains and formed a new Catholic Association. It took some time for the new organization to catch on. During the first few months it was difficult to gather a quorum to hold meetings. Then in 1824, O'Connell

developed the tactics which made the Catholic Association
the model for all popular agitations in Britain and Ireland
during the nineteenth century. He decided that the Association needed a fighting fund and borrowed some of the techniques that the Methodist movement had used to collect
money.[4] Every Catholic parish in Ireland became a unit of
agitation and every priest a recruiting and propaganda agent
for the movement. Full members paid one guinea in dues
every year, but anyone could become an associate member
by contributing a shilling a year in monthly payments of
just one penny. The pennies were collected outside the
church doors on Sunday morning. Strong sermons from the
priests endorsing the methods and goals of the Association
and asking for public support encouraged tenant farmers
and agricultural laborers to contribute to the movement.
The Catholic "rent" not only swelled the treasury of the
Association, but also enlisted the support and the enthusiasm
of the masses. O'Connell had created an organized Irish
Catholic opinion. Impoverished people sacrificed liquor
and tobacco to make their contribution to the Catholic rent,
and this sacrifice committed them to the cause. Irish
nationalism now sustained them; it provided them with a
group identity, hope, a cause, and a meaning to life. O'Connell became the uncrowned king of Ireland, the Liberator
who held the Irish Catholic people in the palm of his
hand.

From the beginning it was clear that the Catholic Association was more than just an agitation to repeal political
restrictions on Catholics. It was a national organization with
leaders demanding a wide variety of reforms, including

---

[4] In the eighteenth century, Methodists developed an effective national
organization of societies divided into districts with members paying a
penny a week dues to the steward of the society. British radicals in the
eighteenth century imitated the example of the Methodist organization,
campaign fund, and outdoor mass meeting to promote a variety of reform
causes. O'Connell borrowed from this example.

ultimately the Repeal of the Union. Catholic Emancipation provided the issue and indicated the method to create a national will. By the end of 1825 the Catholic Association had a war chest of £15,000, safely invested in Government securities. From 1825 on the Catholic Association worried the British Government. O'Connell used constitutional methods and tactics, he told his followers to obey the law, and he condemned violence, arguing that mobilized public opinion was a better and more efficient instrument of reform than revolution. But behind O'Connell's constitutional methods there were revolutionary implications. Never before had the British confronted a mobilized and disciplined Catholic opinion with such high morale and emotional commitment to a cause. And while O'Connell preached nonviolence, he intimidated the Government with the threat of war. He warned British politicians that if they were not prepared to come to terms with a constitutional movement, the Irish masses, now made confident through participation in an agitation, might impatiently turn to other leaders who would adopt physical force methods.

The Government did make several efforts to suppress the Catholic Association. Laws were passed outlawing the movement, but O'Connell used his legal dexterity to reorganize the Association under new names and then expand its activities. It became a committee of grievances and a propaganda agency against tithes and in support of mass education, tenant rights, an expanded suffrage, the secret ballot, and parliamentary reform. Through the means of the Catholic movement, O'Connell had married Irish nationalism to Benthamism. Irish newspapers gave more attention to discussions in the Corn Exchange, the meeting place of the Association, than they did to debates in the British Parliament. In fact, the Catholic Association had become an Irish Catholic Parliament.

The general election of 1826 provided the first test of

strength for the Catholic Association. In Waterford the Association endorsed a pro-Catholic Emancipation Protestant, Villiers Stuart, against Lord George Beresford who had held the seat for twenty years. The priests helped the Association steel the courage of the forty-shilling free-holders to vote against the wishes of their landlords, and the powerful Beresford family suffered a defeat. Waterford was an example which encouraged a number of other constituencies (Louth, Monaghan, Westmeath, Armagh, Cork City, Galway) to make Catholic Emancipation an election issue, and priests successfully competed with landlords for the votes of the forty-shilling freeholders. The victories of 1826 elated the Catholic Association, increased the confidence of the Irish masses in their leaders and their cause, frightened the Irish aristocracy, and increased the anxieties of the Tory Government.

Six months after the election, poor health forced Lord Liverpool to resign as Prime Minister, and George Canning took his place. Since Canning was sympathetic to Catholic Emancipation, O'Connell slowed down the pace of the agitation to give the new Prime Minister time to construct and introduce an Emancipation bill in Parliament. But within a few months Canning was dead, anti-Emancipation Wellington was Prime Minister, and another opponent of the Catholic cause, Sir Robert Peel, was Home Secretary and Government leader in the House of Commons. Wellington appointed C. E. Vesey Fitzgerald, M.P. for Clare, to the presidency of the Board of Trade, forcing him to contest his seat in a by-election.

Fitzgerald was a popular landlord and a friend of Catholic Emancipation, but the Catholic Association decided on a bold strategy. This time there would be a direct assault on Catholic exclusion. A Catholic candidate would confront the new cabinet minister. O'Connell was asked to run and, against his inclinations, was persuaded to accept the invitation of his friends. Engaged in a direct battle with the enemy, the Government threw all of its resources and energy into the campaign, but O'Connell had the priests and the forty-shilling voters. Together they defeated the Government, Fitzgerald, and the landlords of County Clare.

How would Wellington and Sir Robert Peel react to this victory of Irish nationalism? In conscience they opposed Catholic Emancipation, but what were the alternatives to making concessions to Catholic demands? After their great triumph in Clare, would the Irish masses passively look on if a British Government denied them the spoils of victory and crushed the Catholic Association? There was a strong probability that if the Government frustrated the Catholic Emancipation movement, it would encourage the increase of nationalistic sentiment and lead to a powerful agitation for a repeal of the Union. And there was a possibility that the Irish masses might reject O'Connell's constitutional methods and attempt to assert their independence by physical force. In any event, if the Government did not concede Catholic Emancipation the task of governing Ireland would be extremely difficult. And if there was a rebellion in Ireland many pro-Catholic Emancipation M.P.'s in the House of Commons would criticize the Government and extend sympathy to the Irish rebels. In addition, there was much economic and social discontent in Britain, the product of industrialism, and this discontent took the form of rioting, machine breaking, and the demand for parliamentary reform. There was a good chance that rebellion in Ireland would encourage lawlessness and agitation in Britain.

In order to preserve peace and stability in Britain as well as in Ireland, Wellington and Peel decided to ignore British no-Popery opinion and the right wing of their own party and concede Catholic Emancipation. But the Government refused to play the role of good loser. In exchange for Catholic Emancipation the forty-shilling freeholder lost the suffrage (an attempt to maintain the political power of landlords), O'Connell was forced to contest Clare a second time (he won but the expense was considerable), the Catholic Association was outlawed, and Catholic M.P.'s had to take an insulting oath of allegiance before taking their seats in the House of Commons.[5]

Now Catholics could sit in both houses of Parliament and were eligible for all offices in the United Kingdom except those of Regent, Lord Chancellor, and Lord Lieutenant and Lord Chancellor of Ireland. The elimination of the forty-shilling voters meant that the electorate in Ireland was reduced from somewhere over 100,000 to around 16,000. Still it was possible that the Irish Catholic voters could return a substantial number of their coreligionists to the House of Commons. The Duke of Wellington expected Catholic Emancipation to result in sixty Catholic M.P.'s. However, M.P.'s were not paid a salary, and the high cost of political campaigns and the expense of maintaining living quarters in London made parliamentary careers out of reach for most Irish Catholics. As late as 1874, after a considerable extension of the suffrage and the adoption of the

---

[5] Many nationalists who have an unfavorable opinion of O'Connell's influence on Irish nationalism have pointed to the disfranchisement of the forty-shilling freeholders as a betrayal of democracy and nationalism. Indeed, it is difficult to understand O'Connell's surrender on this issue. He did protest publicly, but without enthusiasm and only for appearances. In 1825 he did agree to Catholic Emancipation at the price of Government endowment of Catholic priests (another contradiction of a former position) and the disfranchisement of the forty-shilling freehold vote. At that time, he argued that the forty-shilling vote was a controlled vote and not a democratic opinion. But by 1829 the Catholic Association had demonstrated the nationalistic and democratic potentiality of the peasant electorate. Disfranchisement certainly diminished Repeal possibilities at elections and in Parliament. Perhaps O'Connell did not fight hard in 1829 on the forty-shilling vote because he was unwilling to split the Catholic Association. Certainly many Catholics who wanted Emancipation were not necessarily supporters of political democracy.

secret ballot, a general election returned only forty-nine Catholic M.P.'s from Ireland. But there were always Protestant Irish nationalists and liberals prepared to serve in the House of Commons and promote the interests of their Catholic constituents.

While Catholic Emancipation strengthened the significance of Irish opinion in the House of Commons, it also had an impact on British politics. The Tory party was never the same after the Catholic Emancipation crisis. Ultra-Tories fought concessions to Catholics to the bitter end, and they rallied British no-Popery opinion against the bill. They lost, and they never forgave Peel and Wellington, particularly the former, for betraying Protestant interests. Peel under pressure surrendered his seat for Oxford, and a number of the Ultras began to advocate parliamentary reform because they felt the people were more reliably conservative than the aristocratic Parliament. They charged that Parliament had surrendered to Popery in defiance of public opinion. These Ultras joined the Whigs in 1830 to topple the Wellington regime and clear the way for the reform Parliament. The Ultras, in a pique, were only playing with parliamentary reform because British democracy posed just as much of a threat to their interests as Irish nationalism. Ultra-Tory flirtation with radicalism was a fleeting thing, but their distrust of Peel was permanent. This distrust opened a crack in Tory unity which never completely closed, deepened under the stresses of the 1840's, and finally split the party into reactionary and progressive factions.

Catholic Emancipation also played a role in shaping the character of British Liberalism and Radicalism. The victory of the Catholic Association established valuable examples and precedents for the British left. The methods of the Catholic Emancipation movement became models for popular agitation. Radicals, in the successful campaign for parliamentary reform, imitated O'Connell's tactics for mobilizing public opinion, collecting money, and intimidating the Government. Their political unions strongly resembled the Catholic Association, and they too won a victory by presenting the Government with the alternatives of concession or possible civil war. Later, free traders would borrow O'Connell's tactics in their agitation to repeal the Corn Laws.

The victory of Catholic Emancipation encouraged the growth of democracy beyond the issue of parliamentary reform. In 1829 George IV lost a major battle, and this signified the declining position of the monarchy. Emancipation was also a victory of the House of Commons over the House of Lords. It was the first engagement in a long struggle for political power; a contest that would finally end with the Parliament Act of 1911, another contribution of the Irish Question to the evolution of British democracy.

When they conceded Catholic Emancipation, Peel and Wellington hoped to preserve British institutions by avoiding civil war. They also wanted to frustrate the growth of Irish nationalism by lessening Irish discontent. But the great victory of 1829 did not make the Irish masses feel that they owed a debt to the British Government. Emancipation had been delayed too long and was granted only with humiliating strings attached. Instead of gratitude to Britain, Irish Catholics felt confidence in their united strength. They were encouraged to use the power of disciplined public opinion to demand other reforms: religious equality, tenant right, an expanded suffrage, and eventually an independent Irish parliament. The issue of Catholic Emancipation created Irish nationalism, enhanced O'Connell's prestige and position as leader of the Irish masses, and opened a new era in Irish agitation that would complicate British politics and alter British institutions. And with the rise of an organized

Catholic national opinion, the cleavage between Irish Catholic and Protestant widened. Protestants' anxiety about the continued existence of their ascendancy increased, and they became more passionately committed to the British connection.

CHAPTER TWO

Repeal, 1829-1845

When O'Connell entered the House of Commons in 1829, most of the political experts predicted that he would not succeed in his new venture and consequently would decline as a force in British and Irish political life. They said that since it took years to acquire the techniques and influence to become a leader in the House of Commons, he was too old at fifty-four to launch a parliamentary career. A man had to be a skilled speaker and debater to command the attention of other M.P.'s. O'Connell's demagogic style, which combined earthiness, blarney, exaggeration, and invective, might impress Irish peasants, but it would only antagonize British gentlemen.

The political experts underrated their man. O'Connell was an immediate power in the House of Commons. He worked hard for the interests of his country and played the parliamentary game with unbelievable skill. Occasionally he would become scurrilous in his speeches—a tactic used to bait his opponents and to please the folks back home—but he adjusted his speaking style to the parliamentary situation. Even his enemies had to concede that he was one of the leading debaters in the House of Commons. He had a beautiful speaking voice and used it to present Irish grievances and to plead with passion and reason the case for Irish reform and Repeal of the Union.

In the early 1830's, O'Connell emphasized the Repeal issue, but Tory and Whig Governments were equally determined to frustrate the growth of an effective anti-Union agitation in Ireland. In fact, the Whig administration that took office in 1830 demonstrated more diligence in curtailing Irish nationalism than did Wellington and Peel. Although Whig leaders courted O'Connell's support with offers of Government office, Lord Anglesey, the Lord Lieutenant, and Lord Stanley, Chief Secretary, quickly outlawed every political organization initiated by the Irish leader.

O'Connell deserved much of the credit for the passage of the reform bill in 1832. His influence on that change in the Constitution was both direct and indirect. The Radical leaders who led the agitation in Britain for parliamentary reform modeled their tactics on the ones used by O'Connell in Ireland to win Catholic Emancipation. Their political unions, in organization and methods, were copies of the Catholic Association. In their newspapers they reported and exaggerated discontent in Britain. They warned the Whig Government that there were only two alternatives: parliamentary reform or revolution. Not all of the Whig leaders were convinced that revolution would follow a failure to reform, but like Peel and Wellington in 1829, they could not afford to take a chance.

O'Connell directly aided the cause of parliamentary reform by supporting the bill with public speeches and with the votes he and his Irish followers cast in close divisions in the House of Commons. O'Connell fought for parliamentary reform because he was a democrat and a Benthamite, and because he had hopes that a reformed British Parliament might concede reform and perhaps even Repeal to Ireland. But the final contents of the reform bill disappointed the Repealers.

The Irish reform bill increased the Irish electorate to around 93,000 (less than the pre-1829 total) and raised Irish representation in the House of Commons from 100 to 105. But in proportion to other sections of the United Kingdom, Ireland was shortchanged in political reform. A £10 borough franchise in Ireland did not radically increase the electorate or begin to diminish the influence of the aristocracy. As a result of the reform bill, one person in 115 voted in Irish county elections in contrast to one in twenty-four in England, one in twenty-three in Wales, and one in forty-five in Scotland.[1] In the cities the Irish franchise was one in twenty-two; in England and Wales it was one in seventeen, and in Scotland it was one in twenty-seven. O'Connell insisted that an increase of five M.P.'s in the House of Commons did not adequately represent the quickly expanding Irish population, but British politicians replied that property interests were more important than population in determining Irish influence in Parliament.

Despite his disappointment with the Irish reform bill, O'Connell refused to cut his ties with the Whigs and ignored the condescending manner in which he was treated by Lords Grey and Melbourne and other members of the Whig artistocracy. He believed that the Tories would never desert the cause of Protestant Ascendancy and that the Whigs offered the only possible avenue to Irish reform.

Against his better judgment but under the pressure of Irish nationalist opinion, O'Connell, in 1834, introduced a Repeal motion in the House of Commons. The humiliating results of this effort—only one British M.P. supported the motion—convinced the Irish leader that the British Parlia-

[1] A £10 freehold county suffrage was established with Catholic Emancipation in 1829. In 1832 holders of land worth £10 with a twenty-year lease were added to the county suffrage.

ment would never seriously consider self-government for Ireland until the Repeal cause was supported by an organized, disciplined, massive, and enthusiastic agitation in Ireland.

During the first five years that O'Connell gave Irish nationalist support to the Whig Government, the rewards were meagre. Only Lord Stanley's Irish education bill (1831), which established a state supported system of national education on the primary level, was a significant contribution to Ireland. In order to minimize religious conflict, the national schools offered nondemoninational education in secular subjects, but the various sects could supplement this with religious instruction for the members of their own faith. Protestant leaders objected to the system of "Godless education" which deprived them of a monopoly over Irish education. Most Catholic leaders welcomed the opportunity to raise the cultural level of the Irish masses, but later, when the Catholic hierarchy developed a spirit of boldness and self-confidence, Archbishops Cullen (Dublin), the Ultramontane, and MacHale (Tuam) the nationalist, condemned the national schools. The former said they were instruments of Protestant proselytism; the latter considered them agents of British rule. When Catholics began to attack the national schools, Protestants switched their position and began to defend the system to avoid Government financial aid to denominational schools, which would be mostly Catholic. In fact, by the mid-nineteenth century, the national schools had already become denominational. In Catholic districts the priest was head of the school board, and in Protestant areas the parson performed that function.

However, the national system of education in Ireland had implications for Britain. The Government in Ireland experimented with a system of state supported, theoretically secular education at a time when it was afraid to risk such legislation in Britain. The Irish experiment was a victory for British Radicalism, and it increased pressure for a system of nondenominational state supported education in Britain.

For five years the Whigs enjoyed the benefits of Irish nationalist support without the inconveniences of an open alliance. Then in 1835 the balance of political forces in the House of Commons forced the Whig leaders to come to terms with O'Connell. The Lichfield House Compact, an alliance between Whigs, Radicals, and Irish nationalists, promised O'Connell reforms in the administration of Irish affairs in exchange for his guarantee to keep the Whigs in office and to aid them in their efforts to govern Ireland. In effect, this meant that O'Connell had agreed to abandon the agitation for Repeal in return for a promise of reform. Of course, the Tories denounced the Whig, Radical, Irish combination as a dishonorable and unholy alliance, and some Irish nationalists agreed with this interpretation. Lords Russell and Melbourne replied that there was nothing in the contents of the Lichfield House compact contrary to Whig principles, and O'Connell insisted that his arrangements with the Whigs did not violate his political convictions.

While O'Connell had always preached Repeal, he had no inherent objection to the British connection. He demanded an Irish Parliament because he was convinced that only Irishmen could solve the political, religious, social, and economic problems unique to agrarian, feudal Ireland.[2] The Repeal leader believed that under the Union Irish needs were subordinated to British interests, but he was willing to let British politicians prove him wrong. O'Connell often

[2] Of course O'Connell knew that an Irish House of Commons would be dominated by the Protestant Ascendancy. They were the only class that could afford the luxury of a political career, with its heavy election expenses and service without compensation. Protestants in an Irish Parliament, however, would be influenced by Irish Catholic opinion and a large Irish Catholic electorate. Irish Catholic opinion would have much more influence on a parliament in Dublin than on one at Westminster. And O'Connell expected that time would bring changes and reforms that would increase Catholic representation in a Dublin legislature.

told Irish audiences that he would accept the Union as a permanent arrangement on the following conditions: Britain must treat Ireland as an equal partner, Parliament must discuss Irish issues in Irish and not British terms and give Irish problems a sympathetic hearing, and British Governments must endeavour to promote the prosperity of Ireland.

Except when making speeches to the peasant masses, O'Connell was not a fanatic nationalist. He did not subscribe to the romantic cultural nationalism which developed in the early nineteenth century, first on the Continent, then in Britain, and, with Young Ireland, in his own country. As a disciple of Bentham, he was more interested in the personal liberty, happiness, and economic security of the Irish people than in such abstract concepts as national sovereignty or the folk soul. Though he doubted that the legislature of the United Kingdom, dominated by the representatives of a Protestant country with a booming industrial economy, could ever have the patience, the sympathy, or the understanding to solve the problems of Catholic, agrarian Ireland, O'Connell, in the Lichfield Compact, gave the Whigs another opportunity to prove to Ireland the advantages of the Union.

The Melbourne administration did place three important Irish bills on the statute books. In 1838 the tithe was commuted to a tax on landed property ,thus theoretically freeing Catholic tenant farmers from the obligation of supporting the Protestant church. That same year, the controversial principle of the British poor law—the workhouse test for relief—was applied to Ireland, but the Irish poor law did not go into effect until 1842. The Irish municipal reform bill, which passed through Parliament in 1840, opened Irish city government to Catholic participation. Of these three bills, the poor law is perhaps the best example of the problems of a British Parliament legislating for Ireland.

In 1833 the Prime Minister, Lord Grey, appointed an

Irish commission to investigate the problem of poverty in Ireland and to recommend solutions. This commission, which included prominent Catholic, Protestant, and Presbyterian clergymen, spent two years in collecting and evaluating evidence and submitted its conclusions and recommendations to the Government in 1836. The commission repudiated the British poor law system as a remedy for Irish poverty. In Ireland poverty was not a disgrace, and the pauper had an important role in Irish society. Wandering mendicants brought news and entertainment into peasant cottages and provided people with an opportunity to practice Christian charity. Irishmen would resent the Government locking poor people up in workhouses as if they were guilty of some crime. Ireland could not afford the British poor law system. About two-and-a-half million Irishmen were on the verge of starvation. To place all of them in workhouses would overburden the financial resources of a poor country, and the expense would reduce many others into the ranks of the mendicants. Instead of a poor law, the commission asked the Government for more voluntary relief agencies, public works projects to provide employment and to improve the economic potential of the country, and a program to encourage emigration of the surplus population.

Lord John Russell, the Whig leader in the House of Commons, ignored the report of the Irish poor law commission. His utilitarian logic argued that what was good for Britain was no doubt practical for Ireland. He sent George Nicholls, a British poor law official, to Ireland to conduct another survey on poverty. Nicholls was only in Ireland for six weeks, but he recommended a poor law on the British model, and his recommendation became the law.

O'Connell was not satisfied with the fruits of the Whig alliance. The tithe act failed to meet his demand for the disestablishment of the Protestant Church, and it did not

prevent landlords from raising rents to compensate them for
the tax they paid to the Church. His agreement with the
Whigs prevented him from vigorously opposing the poor
law, although he did vote against it and argued that
it was not appropriate to the Irish situation. O'Connell
also complained that the Whigs did not increase the Irish
parliamentary franchise or Irish representation in the House
of Commons and that they did not do enough to destroy the
Protestant monopoly of power in Dublin Castle.[3]

In 1838 O'Connell decided to warn Melbourne that the
Whigs must earn the support of Irish nationalist M.P.'s.
He organized the Precursor Society as a prelude to the
revival of the agitation for Repeal of the Union and again
demanded substantial Irish reforms. By 1840 it was clear
that the Melbourne administration would not introduce any
more important Irish bills, so O'Connell decided to imple-
ment his threat of 1838. In April 1840 he chaired the first
public meeting of the National Association of Ireland, which
was rechristened the Loyal National Repeal Association in
1841. The new organization met at the Corn Exchange,
Burgh Quay, Dublin. Only a hundred people attended the
first meeting, and just fifteen of them applied for membership. This apathetic response to O'Connell's summons to
action was an indication that many Irish nationalists were
afraid that their leader's alliance with the Whigs revealed
an insincerity concerning Repeal, and that the new organization was only intended as an instrument to force more concessions from a reluctant Melbourne.

O'Connell modeled the Repeal Association on the Cath-

---

[3] Although Whig legislation disappointed O'Connell, Thomas Drummond,
undersecretary at Dublin Castle, curbed the Protestant Ascendancy. He
told landlords that they had duties as well as rights and appointed Catholics
to government, magisterial, and legal positions. Drummond also drove the
Orange Order underground. Orange Societies, named in honor of William
of Orange, had developed around 1795 with the objective of maintaining
Protestant Ascendancy. The liberal and tolerant spirit in the Irish administration died with Drummond in 1840.

olic Association. Members paid one pound in annual dues. Those who contributed ten pounds or more were called Volunteers and could wear a uniform similar to the one worn by the Irish Volunteers in 1782 when they forced concessions from the British Parliament and Government.[4] But O'Connell wanted the same mass support for Repeal that he had had for Catholic Emancipation. To get it, he invited tenant farmers, agricultural laborers, and the urban proletariat to become associate members of the Repeal organization for a shilling a year, paid in weekly installments of a farthing. In urban and rural parishes Repeal wardens, men selected by the local clergy and approved by nationalist leaders in Dublin, collected the dues and sent them, along with the names of the contributors, to Dublin. They also encouraged Repeal enthusiasm in their districts and established reading rooms where Repealers, and those interested in the movement, could read nationalist newspapers and pamphlets. The Repeal warden performed all the functions we now associate with a precinct captain. He was the main cog in the Repeal machinery.

For the first three years of its existence, the Loyal National Repeal Association made little progress in its goal to capture the allegiance of Irish opinion. Most of the energetic and bright Catholic lawyers who had helped O'Connell construct an effective Catholic Emancipation agitation were now successes in their profession. They were reluctant to jeopardize their economic and social standing by supporting an anti-British movement with few prospects of success.

---

[4] During the American Revolution, Britain had to withdraw troops from Ireland for use in North America. With France and Spain allied to the American rebels, other Continental countries neutral but hostile to Britain, and France enjoying a temporary naval supremacy, an invasion of Ireland was possible. Irish patriots organized a volunteer army to defend Ireland. Following American precedents, the patriots used the Volunteers to extort concessions from the British Government. In 1782, the Volunteer leaders forced Britain to remove restrictions on the freedom of the Irish Parliament to legislate for Ireland.

Many of them, like Richard Lalor Sheil, were loyal allies of the Whigs in the House of Commons, and some held Government office. Even the Catholic hierarchy seemed indifferent to the fortunes of Repeal. O'Connell was left with those attached to him through personal loyalty or family ties. He would have to find a new group of lieutenants from a new generation of discontented young men.

On October 15, 1842, the first issue of the *Nation* was published. This nationalist weekly was the product of the combined talents of Thomas Osborne Davis, John Blake Dillon, and Charles Gavan Duffy—three young men in their twenties, trained in the law and experienced in journalism. Davis was an Anglo-Irish Protestant; Dillon and Duffy were Catholics; Davis and Dillon had attended Trinity College; Davis was from Dublin, Dillon from Connacht, and Duffy from Ulster; all three were influenced by liberalism as well as nationalism. Davis, Dillon, and Duffy gave Irish nationalism the most powerful and influential newspaper voice it ever had or ever would have, and they contributed traditions and values that would permanently shape its character.

Duffy, Dillon and Davis began the *Nation* to inspire a cultural nationalist opinion in Ireland: "to create and foster public opinion and make it racy of the soil." They insisted that a nation was a spiritual as well as a geographical entity. A nation must have cultural independence and integrity as well as political sovereignty. The Young Irelanders, as the writers associated with the *Nation* came to be called, defined Irish cultural nationalism, and their definition conquered Irish nationalist opinion. Young Ireland emphasized the spiritual qualities of agrarian Ireland and its peasant people and ridiculed the materalism of urban and industrial Britain. An Irish Parliament would save their country from the contamination of an alien culture. Since the British planned, organized, and controlled Irish national school system tended to destroy the Irish cultural heritage and thus

force Irishmen to adopt British values, Young Ireland under-
took the responsibility of educating Irishmen to know and
appreciate their own history and culture.

The *Nation* attracted the talents of Thomas MacNevin,
Daniel Owen Madden, John Mitchel, John O'Hagan, Thomas
D'Arcy McGee, and Thomas Meagher. These young journalists praised the high standards of early Christian Irish culture
and discussed the contribution made by Irish missionaries
to the spread of civilization in Western Europe. They also
wrote about the Irish patriots who fought Dane, Norman,
and Englishman to preserve Irish independence. The editors
of the *Nation* did more than exalt the past; they also tried
to encourage a cultural revival. They published the best in
contemporary Irish writing—James Clarence Mangan, William Carleton, and other creative writers and scholars contributed to the *Nation*—and they invited their readers to
submit essays, poems, and ballads. Many of the nationalist
songs still enjoying popularity among the Irish at home, in
Britain, the United States, and throughout the Commonwealth first appeared in the *Nation* in the 1840's. A number
of the Young Irelanders were champions of the Irish language. They advocated its preservation where it was still
the language of the people and its revival where it had
declined.

Dillon, Duffy, Davis, and their associates attempted to
divorce Irish nationalism from its close identity with
Catholicism. They pleaded for harmony between Catholics,
Protestants, and Nonconformists and stressed the common
nationality of all Irishmen. In the columns of the *Nation*,
the contributions made by Nonconformists and Protestants
to Ireland received the same attention as the work of Catholics. The *Nation* emphasized the grievances shared by
members of all religions and argued that all Irishmen would
profit by the independence and progress of their common
country.

News coverage played a secondary role to the *Nation's* cultural and propaganda efforts. The editors usually borrowed their news stories from other newspapers. They concentrated Young Ireland's talents on poetry, historical essays, biographical sketches, patriotic ballads, reviews, and editorials. The editorials preached cultural and political nationalism, supported the Repeal movement, encouraged cooperation between religious groups, and advocated tenant right, education for the Irish masses (cultural and vocational), and political reforms consistent with liberalism and democracy. The cultural nationalism preached by the *Nation* had such an immediate impact on Irish national opinion that this newspaper was soon a topic for discussion in Parliament. British M.P.'s praised the talents of Young Ireland, but condemned its revolutionary and anti-British message.

O'Connell welcomed the Young Irelanders to the Loyal National Repeal Association, but he was always a little suspicious of his militant young allies. Since O'Connell's nationalism was rooted in a Benthamite concern for the bread and butter issues of politics, he never really understood the uncompromising cultural nationalism of Young Ireland. On the political platform O'Connell never hesitated to tell the Irish people that they were the most virtuous, handsome, and intelligent people in the world and that they lived in a country unmatched in physical beauty or in economic potential. This was blarney used to lift the spirits of people demoralized by over a century of ignorance, oppression, and poverty.

O'Connell sincerely loved his country and his fellow countrymen, Protestant, Nonconformist, and Catholic, and he was proud of his position as "uncrowned King of Ireland." However he had little time for excursions into the Gaelic past. His utilitarian views are well illustrated by his attitude toward the Irish language. Unlike the Young

Irelanders, he was a native speaker and occasionally used Irish in his political speeches, sometimes to confuse police reporters, but he was opposed to efforts to preserve the language. To him, Irish was a symbol of inferiority and a barrier to progress. O'Connell was so occupied with the future of Ireland that he had little concern for its past. He wanted Irishmen to have all of the cultural and technological advantages of nineteenth-century living. O'Connell did not hate England or English culture. He admired Britain's technological advance, her Constitution, her political institutions, her liberal tradition. He wanted all of these things for his own people.

Since the cosmopolitan O'Connell could not understand or sympathize with the spirit of cultural nationalism which had spread throughout Europe and entered his own country in the form of Young Ireland, he distrusted the militant tone of the *Nation* and sometimes ridiculed its literary efforts. On the other hand, Young Irelanders were often impatient with O'Connell's pragmatism, flirtations with the Whigs, vulgarity, willingness to compromise Repeal for reform, and despotic control over the Repeal Association. The *Nation* and O'Connell disagreed on the Chartists, corn law repeal, and Federalism. Young Ireland viewed the Chartists as representatives of the British democracy and therefore natural allies of Irish nationalists against the common enemy, the British aristocracy. O'Connell condemned the Chartists, particularly his old enemy Fergus O'Connor, for methods of agitation which tended to encourage violence. He was true to his utilitarian, free trade convictions in advocating the repeal of the corn laws. The *Nation* argued that protection was necessary for the welfare of the Irish agrarian economy and that free trade would benefit industrial Britain at the expense of Ireland. Young Ireland was prepared to work with Irish Federalists in a common attack on British domination in Ireland, but it considered the limited Irish Parliament advocated by the Federalists as inadequate for Irish needs. O'Connell was inclined to accept a Federal Constitution as a settlement of Irish claims if he could get British politicians to make such an offer and Irish opinion to accept it.

Despite their differences in temperament, procedure, and policy, Young Ireland realized that O'Connell had the allegiance of the Irish masses and that without him the national movement would collapse. Therefore, they were gentle in their criticism of the old man. They submitted to his leadership in the Loyal National Repeal Association, and their propaganda efforts contributed to the revival of national enthusiasm. About eight thousand people bought the *Nation* every week, but its influence extended beyond this number. The *Nation* was in Repeal reading rooms, and all over the country illiterate peasants crowded into thatch-roofed cottages to listen to the local scholar read the poems, the essays, and the editorials of Young Ireland.

During 1842 Repeal activities were practically suspended while O'Connell served as the first Catholic Lord Mayor of Dublin. When the year 1843 began, he had just completed his term, his old enemy, Sir Robert Peel, was Prime Minister of the Conservative Government, and his organization, the Loyal National Repeal Association was meeting weekly at the Corn Exchange. However, no one in authority considered the Repeal movement a serious threat to British rule in Ireland. Writers in British newspapers and periodicals described O'Connell as a washed-up old demagogue agitating Repeal to keep his name before the Irish masses so he could line his pockets with the contributions of Irish peasants. If this was his motive, he was unsuccessful. The Irish people demonstrated their indifference to self-government by not contributing their farthings and pennies to the Repeal rent. Only the success of the *Nation* indicated that the principle of nationalism retained the loyalty of the Irish masses.

This was frustrating to O'Connell, who loved the limelight, needed the Tribute which he received from the Irish people every year (a financial contribution to compensate him for sacrificing his law practice to work in their interest), still had work to do for Ireland, and could not achieve his goals without the support, financial and moral, of the Catholic masses. So in January 1843 he decided to wage one more campaign for an Irish Parliament or Irish reform, knowing that he had at his disposal the necessary ingredients for a successful agitation.

Although Catholic Emancipation, reform of the municipal corporations, the national schools, and the conversion of the tithe to a rent charge paid by the landlord satisfied some of the needs of Irish national opinion, these concessions to Irish agitation did not diminish Irish discontent because they were half-way measures enacted in a surly and reluctant manner. Poverty, Protestant Ascendancy, and the tenant right issue remained to perpetuate tensions between the British and the Irish. When the Government put the poor law into operation in 1842, all sections of Irish opinion attacked it. Catholic and Protestant leaders united to condemn the workhouse test and the refusal to give outdoor relief. Nationalists, Tories, and Whigs all protested against the despotic powers of the Central Board of Poor Law Commissioners and complained about the expenses of operating a project designed for an industrial rather than an agrarian situation.

Members of the upper and middle classes expressed their disapproval of the poor law in petitions to Parliament, platform speeches, and letters to the editors of newspapers. The masses, however, often resorted to more spectacular and sometimes violent methods. In many sections of the country the people refused to pay poor rates, even when the Government sent the army to collect them. O'Connell recognized how opposition to the poor law stimulated anti-British passions, so he encouraged the protest and included an anti-poor law plank as a major part of his Repeal platform. His strategy paid quick dividends. In the spring of 1843, as the anti-poor law agitation tapered off, the Repeal Association grew in strength, numbers, and financial stability.

In January 1843 the most popular and influential man in Ireland, next to O'Connell, was Theobold Mathew, a Franciscan Friar. Father Mathew had enrolled between four and five million in his Temperance Society. Almost every small town in the country had a local branch of the society, complete with a reading room and a band with colorful uniforms. Even the Protestant Ascendancy dominated newspapers praised Father Mathew's efforts to curb the tendency of the Irish masses to escape the realities of poverty in the bottle and the jug. O'Connell considered the discipline and the enthusiasm of the temperance movement as potential sources of Repeal strength. Father Mathew had continued the tradition of mass meetings and organization that O'Connell created in the 1820's. O'Connell tried to lure the teetotalers and their leaders into the ranks of Repeal by endorsing temperance at Repeal meetings. He described temperance as the most powerful weapon in the Repeal arsenal of moral force. Temperance would discipline nationalists and strengthen them for their struggle against British tyranny.

Father Mathew wanted to avoid partisan politics and refused to alienate Irish and British Protestants by associating temperance with Irish nationalism. He could not, however, control the political loyalties or dictate the political opinions of his followers, and O'Connell succeeded in his strategy to capture the discipline, the enthusiasm, and the organizational experience of the teetotalers for his movement. During the Repeal agitation of 1843 temperance bands played an important role at political meetings, and the *Nation* was read in temperance reading rooms.

After O'Connell had maneuvered the anti-poor law agitation and the temperance movement into the paths of Repeal, he persuaded the Dublin Corporation, along with other municipal and public bodies, to petition Parliament for a Repeal of the Union. Then Government officials helped him mobilize Irish opinion behind the demand for an Irish Parliament by a series of tactical blunders. They awarded the Irish mail-coach contract to a Scottish company in preference to an Irish concern already holding the concession, thus forcing thousands of Dublin workers to face the prospect of unemployment in an already job-starved city. Then Dr. Phelan, the only Catholic involved in the administration of the poor law, was dismissed from his Government post without an explanation. And when the Government finally decided to amend the poor law, concessions were made to the demands of the gentry while the protests of the masses were ignored.

During the heat of the Repeal agitation the government pushed through Parliament an Irish arms bill which curtailed civil liberties, and the Irish Lord Chancellor, Sir Edward Sugden, dismissed magistrates attending Repeal meetings, although he conceded that the meetings were legal and constitutional. The arms bill and the dismissal of the magistrates rallied Catholic barristers and solicitors to the Repeal standard and gave O'Connell the support of an influential segment of the Catholic middle class that had largely deserted him after the achievement of Catholic Emancipation.

In the spring of 1843 O'Connell began to hold a series of public meetings to petition for a Repeal of the Union, choosing a different part of the country every week. The meetings were held on Sunday afternoons. Hundreds of thousands came to hear the Liberator speak. Early Sunday mornings the roads were crowded with Repealers who had journeyed many miles to attend the meeting. Outdoor

Masses were said by priests on the hillsides. When the religious service was over, the people sat down to eat their breakfasts of potatoes. Priests, temperance bands, local dignitaries, and lines of marching Repealers met O'Connell's carriage as it approached the town. They detached the horses and pulled the carriage by hand through the streets as women and children threw flowers at the Liberator.

At the meeting, O'Connell told his audience that they were the bravest, strongest, most patient, most virtuous people in the world. Before the year was out they would have their own Parliament in Dublin. They would win this victory through moral force. They would never fight unless attacked. Peel and Wellington would surrender to Irish national opinion as they did in 1829. After Ireland had her own legislature, Irishmen would solve the problems confronting their country. Tenant farmers would be secure on their farms, trade and commerce would flourish, and culture would thrive. Catholics, Protestants, and Nonconformists would live in harmony. There would be freedom of conscience with no established church. A free Ireland loyal to the Crown would live in peace with Britain. O'Connell always encouraged loyalty to the Queen. He assured his listeners that if her ministers "Orange Peel" and "stunted corporal" Wellington denied the Irish people justice, Victoria would use the Royal prerogatives to establish the Irish Parliament. In preparation for independence, O'Connell promised to summon a pre-Parliament, the Council of Three Hundred, to Dublin and to establish arbitration courts so that the Irish people could seek justice in Irish rather than in British courts. By the fall of the year the arbitration courts were operating with surprising effectiveness.

The Monster Meetings, as they were called, were tremendous successes. They stimulated Repeal enthusiasm, and Repeal dues poured into the association treasury. There were five weeks during the late spring and summer when the Repeal rent exceeded £2,000. Much of this money came from the Irish in Britain and the United States, although Irish Americans in the southern states were bitter when O'Connell denounced slavery in the United States and those Irish-Americans who supported such a vile institution. O'Connell was ahead of his time in not only demanding emancipation of slaves, but full political and civil rights for Negroes, fellow sons and daughters of God and equal members of the human race.

The Monster Meetings and the size of the Repeal rent frightened Irish Protestants. They feared an attack on their privileged position and an end of the Union which protected that position. They demanded that the Government suppress the Repeal agitation and outlaw the Loyal National Repeal Association. Earl DeGrey, the anti-Catholic Lord Lieutenant, supported their plea.

Peel and even DeGrey were strangely unaware of the gradual but steady increase of Repeal enthusiasm during the early spring of 1843. Not until May did the Prime Minister realize that O'Connell had mobilized a formidable challenge to British authority in Ireland. As soon as he recognized the challenge Peel told Parliament that he would preserve the Union at all costs, but he found it difficult to deal directly with the Repeal agitation. Legislation designed to suppress the Loyal National Repeal Association would also embrace the Anti-Corn Law League, which followed O'Connell's formula for a popular agitation. An attack on Repeal might unite Radicals, democrats, free traders, and Irish nationalists in a common crusade in defense of civil and political liberties. This would make O'Connell respectable in Britain and both the anti-corn law and Repeal agitations more difficult to control.

Since Peel had to reject anti-Repeal strategy which might provide O'Connell with British allies, he was forced to treat revitalized Irish nationalism with a policy of calculated indifference. His refusal to respond with coercive legislation or military force to O'Connell's boasts and militant posturing infuriated the reactionary, anti-Irish, no-Popery core of the Conservative party, but his indifference masked a carefully cultivated scheme to destroy O'Connell's influence in Ireland and to eradicate the roots of Irish nationalism. By refusing to acknowledge the significance of Repeal by either coercion or immediate conciliation, Peel hoped to demonstrate to the Irish masses that the scarcely veiled threats of the Repeal agitation would not intimidate the Government into conceding Repeal or reform. He hoped that once the nationalist rank and file realized that O'Connell could not redeem any of his extravagant pledges, they would lose confidence in him and his methods of agitation. Repeal would then dwindle into insignificance, and the British army could easily handle any Irish hotheads who dared try to destroy the Union by force of arms.

While Peel and Sir James Graham, the Home Secretary, waited for their tactic of indifference to deflate the balloon of Repeal, they planned a long range Irish policy to satisfy some of the needs and ambitions of the various components of the Repeal coalition and thus destroy nationalism by eliminating the grievances which created and nourished it. The Government, however, had no intention of initiating reforms while Repeal was at white heat and O'Connell enjoyed the confidence of the Irish masses. Concessions to Irish demands in 1843 might encourage nationalists to believe that the Government was susceptible to intimidation and O'Connell to intensify agitation. Peel wanted an Irish policy that was more than a fearful and ill-considered response to Irish discontent. He wanted to lay the Irish Question permanently to rest and to make the Union between the two islands a true community of interests and loyalties.

Of course, there was the danger that O'Connell, faced with the necessity to maintain his influence over the Irish masses, would commit himself to a revolutionary conspiracy. There was also the possibility that he might lose the reins of Irish nationalism to a more militant faction of the Repeal party. So Peel and Graham took out an insurance policy against the failure of their Irish strategy. Troops, weapons, ammunition, and supplies were dispatched to Ireland, and arms were stored for possible use by the Protestant yeomen. The Prime Minister and his Home Secretary were also determined that O'Connell and his chief lieutenants would suffer the consequences of their audacious challenge to British authority. Graham instructed the Irish law officers to collect evidence against the Repeal agitators that would justify prosecutions for sedition.

When Peel told Parliament in May that he was ready if necessary to use military force to maintain the Union, and when Sugden acted on this declaration by dismissing Repeal magistrates, O'Connell was convinced that the Government would employ coercion to smash Repeal. In an effort to make Peel reconsider, and to maintain the enthusiasm and confidence of his supporters, he adopted a militant tone in his speeches to the Irish masses. He even went so far as to suggest that he was prepared to lead the forces of Irish nationalism in a defensive war against Her Majesty's army.

By late summer, however, O'Connell realized that Peel was out to destroy Repeal by undermining the confidence of Irish nationalists in their leader's ability to deliver on his promises of freedom and reform. He feared that if Peel's strategy succeeded, they might turn to physical force and reject the methods of constitutional agitation. And to protect his people from the bullets and bayonets of British soldiers, O'Connell softened the tone of his public statements. He no longer promised Repeal in the near future. He said it would be impossible to summon the Council of Three Hundred before the year was out. Instead of promising quick victories, O'Connell now asked Irish nationalists to support him in a long struggle for freedom. He warned against men who counseled violence and insisted that moral force would eventually triumph over anti-Irish British opinion.

By early autumn it was apparent that Peel's patience was achieving its objectives. O'Connell was preparing his followers for frustration, the Repeal rent had declined, and Irish tenant farmers were neglecting agitation to concentrate their energies on an abundant harvest. Now that the enemy was in retreat, Peel made preparations to assume the offensive. He decided to prosecute the Repeal leaders for sedition and sent Lord DeGrey and Sugden to Dublin to supervise the arrest and prosecution of O'Connell and his lieutenants. They were also instructed to prevent the Clontarf Repeal meeting scheduled for Sunday, October 8. This was to be the last of the Monster Meetings in 1843. A tremendous crowd was expected to gather in the Dublin suburb; even Repealers from the Irish communities in Britain were crossing the Irish sea for the event.

Late Saturday afternoon, October 7, DeGrey issued a proclamation outlawing the Clontarf meeting because the original notice of the meeting—written and distributed when O'Connell was not in Dublin—indicated that it was designed as a military demonstration to intimidate the Government. O'Connell, rather than risk a massacre, canceled the meeting. A week later, he, along with six others (including Charles Gavan Duffy), was arrested and charged with sedition and attempting to subvert the loyalty of soldiers stationed in Ireland. In February 1844 the Repeal defendants were convicted, fined, and sentenced to a year in prison. In September of that same year the Law Lords reversed this decision on the grounds that the prosecution had drawn up an improper indictment and tried its case before a packed jury. O'Connell and his friends were released from Richmond Gaol and received as heroes by the Irish masses. After his prison experience O'Connell seemed to have little zest for agitation.

His decision to abandon the Clontarf meeting and his failure to exploit his legal vindication by intensifying nationalist activity did much to crush the Repeal spirit in Ireland and to undermine confidence in constitutional methods of agitation. But the defeat of O'Connell and Repeal in 1843 was not produced by cowardice or faulty tactics so much as by the Irish leader's misreading of the temper of the times.

Like most political leaders, O'Connell was a captive of his past successes. He expected Peel and Parliament to react to the support of the Irish masses for Repeal in the same way they had to the Catholic Emancipation agitation of the 1820's. Then he had convinced the Tory leaders that if they did not concede Catholic rights, the extremist element in Ireland might push him aside, take control of the movement, and then substitute physical for moral force. In 1843 he seemed to assume that if Peel was again faced with the alternatives of concessions to Irish nationalist opinion or the chaos of rebellion, he would follow the precedent of 1829 and select the former. And if Peel refused to again bow his knee to expediency, O'Connell hoped that the Whig leaders in the House of Commons would exploit the Irish crisis to embarrass and perhaps topple the Conservative Government. Once in power, Russell and Palmerston would probably try to quiet troubled Irish waters with a policy of conciliation and a renewal of the Irish nationalist-Whig alliance.

O'Connell apparently failed to understand that while the situation in Ireland in 1843 was similar to the one prevailing in 1829, in Britain things were quite different. All through the 1820's there was a considerable body of enlightened parliamentary opinion favorable to Emancipation. In 1829 Peel and Wellington knew that any attempt to suppress the Catholic Association without conceding Emancipation would not command majority support in the House of Commons. Therefore, an Irish revolutionary movement in resistance to Government despotism and coercion would enjoy the sympathy of a respectable body of British opinion, and the seeds of rebellion might spread to and take root in a Britain already saturated with social, political, and economic discontent. Catholic Emancipation was an Irish issue with British implications, and the Government's responsibility to preserve peace and order throughout the United Kingdom necessitated a compromise of Protestant principles and a surrender to the demands of Irish Catholic opinion.

But in 1843 no respectable Tory, Whig, or Radical M.P. accepted Repeal as a satisfactory solution to the Irish Question. Both Tories and Whigs argued that an independent Ireland would weaken Britain's defenses and prepare the way for a dissolution of the Empire. Tories also insisted that Repeal would place the democratic Catholic masses in a position to take revenge on the Irish Protestant minority. Radical leaders maintained that the Union, if properly managed, could bring peace and economic prosperity to Ireland. During the Repeal crisis of 1843 British no-Popery and Unionist parliamentary opinion were leagued in opposition to Irish nationalism. Whig and Radical leaders did not hesitate to exploit Irish discontent to embarrass the Conservative Government, but Peel could count on their support in his determination to preserve the Union.

When Peel challenged O'Connell on the issue of the Clontarf meeting, the Irish leader had no realistic choice but to retreat. His nonviolent convictions, his commitment to constitutional methods of agitation, and his common sense would not permit him to lead the Irish masses to slaughter in a futile insurrection against disciplined British troops. When he surrendered to the Government ultimatum O'Connell removed the most effective weapon from the arsenal of constitutional agitation—the implied threat of revolution if the Government refused to submit to the demands of public opinion.

By the beginning of 1844 Peel and Graham were confident

that Repeal was no longer a significant threat and, therefore, it was time to translate their comprehensive Irish policy into legislation. Although this policy included concessions to each of the clerical, agrarian, and middle class components of the nationalist coalition, its main purpose was to detach the priests from popular agitation. Peel accepted a thesis popular in British intellectual and political circles that Irish priests were forced to promote anti-Union activities because they were dependent on the ignorant anti-British masses for financial support. Before the priest could be persuaded to abandon political agitation, he must be guaranteed another source of income for himself and his church. But separating the clergy from the ranks of nationalism presented many risky problems. If the task was not handled with tact and superb diplomacy, it would alienate British no-Popery opinion, the reactionary Tory element in the Conservative party, the Irish Catholic hierarchy and clergy, and even the Vatican.

The Government began its operation by asking the Pope, Gregory XVI, to condemn the nationalist activities of Irish bishops and priests. Metternich, realizing the implications for all Europe of a radical nationalist hierarchy and clergy in Ireland, was persuaded to endorse the British request.[5] The British emissary to the Vatican told the Pope that if his Government could obtain the support of the Catholic Church in Ireland for efforts to maintain the Union and social order, Peel's Irish policy might culminate in the endowment of

[5] The British, in their successful effort to persuade Metternich to ask the Pope for a condemnation of clerical political activities in Ireland, emphasized the potential danger of the Irish situation for political stability all over Europe. In other European countries, religion was an instrument used by governments to maintain order, but in Ireland the Catholic clergy were instruments of radical and nationalist agitation. The Irish example might inspire similar responses. In the Hapsburg Empire many ethnic groups experienced the same frustrations as Irish Catholics under British rule, and they might start learning from Irish agitations. If Metternich helped the British sever the Catholic clergy from the Irish national movement, he would serve the long range interests of his own empire.

Roman Catholicism in Ireland. Vatican officials welcomed this possibility and the opportunity to establish friendly relations with Whitehall, so Cardinal Fransoni, Prefect of Propaganda, wrote to the Irish hierarchy advising them to cease political activities and to concentrate their energies on spiritual matters. But Fransoni's advice was accepted by only a small minority of the bishops.

In the fall of 1844 the Government initiated the legislative phase of its Irish policy with a bill repealing legislation which prevented or hindered the Catholic Church from inheriting or bequeathing property. The charitable bequests act was intended as a demonstration of the Government's intention to do justice to Catholic interests. In addition, Peel also hoped to use the Catholic bishops on the charitable bequests board, which was established by the act, as agents in an effort to persuade Catholic clerical and middle class opinion that cooperation with the British Government promised more benefits than anti-Union agitation.[6]

In the spring of 1845 the Government made another overture to the Catholic clergy when it introduced a proposal to increase the annual grant to the Roman Catholic seminary at Maynooth and convert it to a permanent endowment. The seminary was established by the Irish Parliament in the 1790's, and the British Government believed it had an obligation to continue financial support for the institution. Yet, every year when the grant came up for renewal, it provoked a wave of anti-Catholic protest which embittered relations

---

[6] O'Connell condemned the charitable bequests act because its provisions were inadequate and because it gave the British Government an opportunity to exert influence over the hierarchy and clergy. Archbishop MacHale and a number of other bishops also attacked the bill. Archbishop Murray of Dublin and a few other prelates accepted the bill and agreed to sit on the charitable bequests board. The conflict within the ranks of the hierarchy emphasized a split which began with a debate over the national education system in the 1830's. Murray viewed the national schools as imperfect but still a progressive influence in Irish life. MacHale and his friends wanted an open system of endowed Catholic education. The feud in the hierarchy was bitter, and both sides frequently appealed to Rome.

between Britain and Ireland. Peel hoped that the Maynooth bill would remove the seminary as an annual issue and at the same time convince the Catholic bishops of the friendly attitude of the Government, thereby smoothing the way for a more extensive endowment of Irish Catholicism. However, the hostility of British no-Popery opinion, in and out of Parliament, to the bill and its long range implications alienated Irish Catholic opinion and made certain that the Government would approach further endowment with cautious and timid steps. Nevertheless, Peel courageously resisted the pressures of Protestant prejudice so prominent among Tories, and with the support of the Whigs passed the Maynooth bill.

The Prime Minister then directed his attention to the educational needs of the Irish Catholic middle class. An Irish colleges bill established three provincial colleges in Ireland. They were organized on the principle of nondenominational or mixed education. It was hoped that in a university environment Protestants and Catholics would mingle and develop a middle class solidarity. Peel thought that exposure to secular culture might emancipate middle class Catholics from nationalism and clericalism by making them realize that they had interests independent of their religion and more important than Repeal. In Britain the colleges bill met a minimum of opposition, but in Ireland O'Connell attacked mixed education as anti-Catholic in spirit and forced the hierarchy to condemn the bill's provisions.[7] Because O'Connell's position on the colleges bill was inconsistent with his

[7] In 1847 and 1848, on the urging of MacHale, the Pope condemned the Queens Colleges. In 1850, at the Synod of Thurles, with Archbishop Cullen presiding, the Irish hierarchy forbade Catholics to attend the Queens Colleges or to accept teaching or administrative posts in them. The next year Rome endorsed the decision of the Irish bishops. In the 1850's Cullen established a Catholic University in Dublin, with John Henry Newman as its first rector. Newman could not get along with the anti-intellectual Irish bishops and returned to England. The Catholic University continued to exist, but Cullen could not get a Government endowment. By rejecting the Queens Colleges, the Irish hierarchy denied their countrymen the educational opportunities they so badly needed.

principles concerning freedom of conscience and Catholic-Protestant harmony, he probably used the education issue as a tactic to preserve Irish nationalism. The Young Ireland faction in the Repeal Association endorsed mixed education because they were convinced that Catholic-Protestant contacts would strengthen nationalism and promote the cultural progress of their country. This conflict over education was the beginning of a feud between Young Ireland and O'Connell, a quarrel which eventually led to the secession of the former from the Repeal Association.

The colleges bill was the last portion of Peel's Irish policy to pass through Parliament. He attempted to conciliate the Irish peasant masses by appointing the Devon Commission to investigate landlord-tenant relations in Ireland and then recommend legislation. Lord Stanley introduced a bill in the House of Lords based on the findings of the commission and designed to introduce a moderate tenant right, but the Government withdrew from the legislative contest when many Whig and Conservative leaders indicated that they would not tolerate even a minor limitation on property rights.

In many areas Peel's Irish policy achieved its desired results. The Vatican had condemned the nationalist activities by bishops and priests, and several of the former cooperated with the Government's efforts to lighten the financial burdens of their church. The charitable bequests board gave Peel the opportunity to continue negotiations with the bishops in his effort to demonstrate to them the potential benefits of the Union. And despite the no-Popery response to the Maynooth bill, the Catholic hierarchy and clergy appreciated Peel's generous intentions and his courage in the face of British anti-Catholicism. Finally, although the colleges bill was condemned by O'Connell and the bishops, it did create a conflict within Irish nationalism, an ideological clash between Young and Old Ireland which eventually destroyed the unity of the Repeal movement.

But Peel's achievements were limited by O'Connell's success in frustrating many of the objectives of his Irish policy. During the debate over the merits of the charitable bequests act, O'Connell told the Irish people that the British Government was attempting to conclude an arrangement with the Vatican at the expense of Irish liberty. O'Connell's tactics forced the bishops to publish the Fransoni message to the Irish hierarchy, intensifying distrust of the British and injuring the status of the Vatican with Irish opinion, and it forced Archbishop Murray of Dublin and British officials to deny any intention of concordat between the British Government and the Roman Catholic Church. By emphasizing the danger of an understanding between Whitehall and Rome, O'Connell, to a certain extent, repaired the breach in Catholic nationalist unity opened by Peel's Irish policy and made the hierarchy cautious about considering endowment by the British Government. He was also aided in his effort to maintain solidarity in the ranks of Irish nationalism when British no-Popery opinion attacked the Maynooth bill, thus demonstrating that Peel's generosity was not a reflection of British popular attitudes toward the Irish. Even the split in Repeal ranks over the colleges bill did not appear fatal in 1845. Old and Young Ireland were still in basic agreement on the aims and methods of agitation.

Of course it is impossible to evaluate the success of Peel's Irish policy by the only valid historical test—its influence on the course of Anglo-Irish affairs. In 1845 the potato blight devastated the Irish economy, provoking agrarian crime and discontent and forcing Peel to abandon, at least for a time, his effort to assimilate Ireland into the British system. Peel used the Famine as an argument in his case against the Corn Laws. Although he indicated concern for the plight of the starving peasant masses, the Prime Minister, confronted with agrarian crime, decided to substitute a policy of coercion for one of conciliation. In June of 1846 he introduced a coercion bill in the House of Commons. On the evening of June 29, the same day Corn Law Repeal passed through the House of Lords, protectionist Tories, in a vengeful mood, joined Whigs, Radical, and Irish nationalists in defeating Peel on Irish coercion, destroying his Conservative Government. But the dispute over the Corn Laws only emphasized a split in the Conservative party that began with Catholic Emancipation and was intensified by Peel's concessions to Irish Catholics.

Since Peel's abortive effort to destroy Irish nationalism had contributed to the fall of his Government, no British leader dared confront the Irish Question in all of its complexity until Gladstone took office in 1868. By that time Irish nationalism had assumed an identity independent of the economic, political, and religious grievances which created and nourished it, and Britain had already forfeited the opportunity "to kill Home Rule with kindness."

CHAPTER THREE

Famine, Revolution, Republicanism, 1845-1870

O'Connell's short stay in prison was as comfortable as the situation permitted, but after his release he seemed to have lost much of his zest for nationalist agitation. He was approaching seventy, and some historians have argued that his personal and political conduct showed signs of senility. There can be no doubt that O'Connell after 1843 was no longer a robust and energetic democratic leader, but he still proved a clever tactician in his attempts to sabotage Peel's Irish policy and in his successful effort to drive the Young Irelanders out of the Repeal Association. The conflict between O'Connell and Young Ireland reached its conclusion in July 1846, when the latter, led by William Smith O'Brien and Charles Gavan Duffy (Davis had died in 1845), walked out of Conciliation Hall rather than agree to the proposition that no situation would justify the use of force in the struggle for Irish freedom.[1]

The pacifist resolution was engineered by O'Connell to rid the Repeal Association of the bright young men who criticized his tactics and by so doing challenged his leadership. Actually, the Young Irelanders were constitutional nationalists, and revolution would remain an academic question until 1848. The Young Irelanders, rigid ideological cultural nationalists, had always been uncomfortable in their alliance with the pragmatic leader of the Irish masses. When O'Connell came out of prison and began flirting with Federalism as an alternative to Repeal, attacked the colleges bill, and finally resumed his collaboration with the Whigs, Young Irelanders, in the *Nation* and in the Loyal National Repeal Association, criticized what they considered a cynical betrayal of nationalist principles.

Relations between nationalism and Catholicism was another issue at stake in the contest between O'Connell and Young Ireland. Most Young Irelanders were Catholics, but they believed it was time to cut the close ties that bound the Catholic hierarchy and clergy to the Repeal movement. They argued that the association between the nationalist organization and the Catholic Church antagonized Irish Protestants and obstructed the creation of a nationalist agitation that would unite Catholics and Protestants in a common effort to destroy British rule in Ireland. They worked for a nationalist movement that was Irish, not Catholic or Protestant. O'Connell was a Benthamite, a believer in freedom of conscience and separation of Church and State, but he was also a master politician committed to reality before theory. He asked Protestants to join him in his attempts to win Irish reform and to Repeal the Union. His ideal was a nationalist movement separate from sectarian considerations, but he could not ignore the fact that he used the Catholic cause to create Irish nationalism, and he doubted if nationalism was yet strong enough to exist independent of its Catholic roots. In this struggle with Young Ireland, the O'Connell faction

---

[1] William Smith O'Brien, a Protestant landlord from Clare, had attempted to win justice for Ireland in the House of Commons. In 1843 he decided that Irish interests would always be sacrificed to British interests in the British Parliament. When O'Connell and his colleagues were arrested in October 1843, O'Brien joined the Loyal National Repeal Association and was its acting leader while O'Connell was in prison.

did not hesitate to use Young Ireland's criticism of the alliance between nationalism and Catholicism to portray the young men as secularists and anticlericals. This tactic turned most of the members of the clergy in the Repeal Association against O'Brien, Duffy, and their followers.

The Young Irelanders in January 1847 set up a rival to the Loyal National Repeal Association. Their Irish Confederation had most of the talent, but the O'Connell family over at Conciliation Hall had the numbers. Most Irish nationalists followed their priests'in remaining loyal to the Liberator and "Old Ireland". This quarrel that split Irish nationalism was certainly ill timed. It occurred when Ireland was going through the greatest crisis in her unfortunate history.

In 1845 a potato fungus that first appeared in North America arrived in Ireland from Europe, causing a Famine that persisted until 1851. Since they had to sell their grain crops and livestock to pay excessive rents, the Irish masses depended on the potato as their sole means of sustenance. From 1845 to 1851 at least a million and a half people starved to death or died from diseases associated with hunger —cholera, fever, and scurvy; many millions more approached the gates of death; and at least another million crossed the Atlantic in fever-filled coffin ships or swarmed across the Irish sea to Cardiff, Glasgow, and Liverpool.

Irish nationalists in the nineteenth century argued—there are still Irishmen and Irish-Americans who hold this view— that Ireland suffered so much and lost so many people because the British Government used the Famine to solve the Irish Question by exterminating a large proportion of the Irish population. This is too simple an explanation of a complex situation. Most of the suffering was a consequence of an inefficient and unproductive agricultural system that existed before the Union. Death, disease, and emigration were also the products of a population explosion produced by the agricultural system and a potato diet. When the

Famine began to decimate the Irish population, British officials in Ireland worked beyond ordinary human capacity to mitigate the disaster. They often contributed money from their own pockets to feed the Irish poor. A number of British physicians fell victims of fever while treating sick Irishmen. People in Britain, including the Queen and members of the royal family, contributed to Famine relief. British religious groups, particularly the Quakers, raised money, ministered to the sick, and distributed food to the hungry.[2] The Government spent a fortune attempting to mitigate the consequences of the Famine. In the first year the Peel administration spent £8,000,000 in relief efforts.

But the Whig Government's reaction to the crisis did give Irish nationalists an excuse to raise the charge of genocide. In a period when the Irish masses were dying of hunger and disease or were going into exile, the United Kingdom was the most prosperous country in the world. The British Government refused to use the full resources of Britain and her wealthy Empire to save its Irish partners in the Union. Committed to laissez faire dogmatism, British politicians did not provide enough food to meet immediate demands or design public works projects to stimulate the Irish economy. Government officials argued that Famine relief should not interfere with normal commercial activity, compete with private business, discourage personal initiative, make the Irish people psychologically dependent on Government handouts, or interfere with private property or private responsibility. In the darkest hours of the Famine Nassau Senior, a prominent economist high in the confidence of the Whig administration, lamented that in 1848 only a million people would die from Famine causes, and that would not be a sufficient number to solve the population problem.

[2] All Protestants, however, were not as charitable as the Quakers. Sometimes Protestants refused to give food to Catholics unless they changed religions. This situation is the source of the Irish term souper—a man who sells his convictions for a bowl of soup.

Charles Edward Trevelyan, Under Secretary of the Treasury
and the man most responsible for the Government's relief
measures, thundered that the Famine was a Divine punishment on the wicked, perverse Irish people.

In many ways, the Irish during the Famine suffered an
experience similar to the one that the Jews would encounter
a century later. Both peoples were victims of ideological
murder. Certainly the Nazis were more ruthless, heartless,
and consistent in the application of racist principles than
Trevelyan and his colleagues were in enforcing the dogmas
of political economy. But an Irishman dying of hunger or
crowded into the bowels of an emigrant ship in the 1840's
would have had scant consolation in knowing that his predic-
ament was not the result of race hate, but the price he must
pay to maintain a free enterprise economy.

The Famine was probably the most significant event in
nineteenth-century Irish history: it destroyed whatever
chance Peel's Irish policy had of soothing Irish Catholic
opinion, left the Irish with bitter memories and an intense
hatred of Britain, emotions they would pass on to their
children and grandchildren, pushed the agrarian issue into
the forefront of the Irish Question, and altered the direction
of Irish nationalism and the complexion of Irish politics.

O'Connell returned to the Whig alliance in 1845. He
helped the Whigs depose Peel in 1846 and then gave the
Russell administration his loyal support. Still the years of
service that O'Connell gave to the Whigs were not adequately rewarded. In the 1830's he had kept them in office
and helped push their legislation through the House of
Commons. The Whigs repaid O'Connell by cheating Ireland
in the reform bill and proposing solutions to Irish problems
concerning tithes, municipal government, and poverty that
were either too conservative, inadequate, or unsuitable for
the Irish situation. Through it all O'Connell retained confidence in the Whigs as the only realistic hope for Irish reform,

and in the Famine crisis he again turned to them for help. In February 1847, as a fading old man with a voice not much louder than a whisper, he rose in the House of Commons and begged the British people to help his starving country. British M.P.'s listened with attention, then ignored the old man's pleas. Broken hearted and close to death, O'Connell set out for Rome in late March of 1847. In Paris he received the homage of French liberals who wanted him to know how much he had contributed to the advance of liberalism and democracy. O'Connell never reached Rome. He died in Genoa on May 15, 1847. His heart was buried in Rome. His body rests in Dublin's Glasnevin cemetery, underneath a gigantic round tower.

While O'Connell created modern Irish nationalism and designed the tactics of constitutional agitation used by the Irish and other peoples in the nineteenth and twentieth centuries, he left Irish nationalism in a shattered state. His alliance with the Whigs split the Repeal movement into Young and Old Ireland factions and destroyed what remained of the Repeal party in the House of Commons. The inadequate returns from the Whig alliance, the defeat of the Repeal agitation in 1843, and the devastation of the Famine weakened the appeal of O'Connell's style of nationalism and left the field to the cultural nationalism of Young Ireland.

After his father's death, John O'Connell took command of the Repeal Association. He inherited the electoral machinery developed by his father and the loyalty of the Catholic clergy. Unfortunately, he did not inherit his father's charm, warm personality, or political genius, so the influence of the Repeal Association continued to decline. Meanwhile, the Young Irelanders in the Irish Confederation were divided on tactics. The principal adversaries were John Mitchel and Charles Gavan Duffy.

John Mitchel, a Unitarian from Ulster and a barrister by training, first contributed to the *Nation* in 1842 and three

years later accepted Duffy's invitation to join its staff as
assistant editor. With the other Young Irelanders, he seceded from the Repeal Association in 1846 and helped
establish the Irish Confederation. By 1847 he had lost
confidence in the tactics of constitutional agitation and in
Young Ireland's goal of enlisting the Protestant gentry in
the nationalist movement. Mitchel believed that the Protestant gentry placed their property interests above the independence of their country. He argued that landlordism was
a bulwark of the Union and should be destroyed, and that
the property of Ireland should be distributed among the
people of Ireland. Mitchel insisted that a strong nationalist
movement had to be based on an agitation for tenant rights.

Mitchel's new convictions were inspired by the writings
of James Fintan Lalor. Lalor came from a family prominent
in nationalist politics. His father, Patrick Lalor, was active
in the anti-tithe agitation of the 1830's, and his younger
brother Peter was a Repealer who later emigrated to Australia where he won a reputation as a labor leader and as a
Minister in the Government of Victoria. James Fintan
Lalor did not share his family's enthusiasm for Repeal. He
believed that a solution of the land question deserved
priority over the demand for an Irish Parliament. In 1843
he wrote Peel advising the Prime Minister that Repeal
could be destroyed by concessions to the needs of tenant
farmers. Duffy was impressed with Lalor's intellect and his
powerful journalistic style and in 1847 invited him to publish
his views. In a series of letters to the *Nation* Lalor expressed
his opinion that the land question was more important than
Repeal and argued that the only way Irish nationalism could
retain mass support was by endorsing the cause of the tenant
farmers. He ridiculed O'Connell's tactics of agitation and
his distinctions between legal and illegal methods. Since
the British Parliament defined what was legal and illegal,
constitutional nationalism would always be limited in its

methods by restrictions imposed by the enemy. He insisted that Irishmen should base their tactics on only one considera- tion, the best interests of their own country, and he suggested a method that would at the same time paralyze British rule in Ireland and destroy landlordism—an agitation against the payment of rent. Mitchel was impressed with Lalor's logic and in early 1848 recommended a variation of his strategy, a campaign against the payment of poor rates.

William Smith O'Brien, with his landlord background, was shocked by the radical proposals of Lalor and Mitchel. He believed that such wild talk would destroy the Confedera- tion's chances of persuading the Protestant gentry to join the national movement. Duffy agreed with O'Brien, Mitchel resigned from his position with the *Nation,* and the two journalists took the conflict over nationalist tactics to the Confederation for a decision. The editor of the *Nation* recommended the formation of an independent parliamen- tary party to publicize Irish grievances and convert British parliamentary and public opinion to the justice of Repeal.[3] If the Irish party failed to make an impression on the British parliament, and if British opinion remained hostile to Irish reforms, then Irish M.P.'s should retaliate by obstructing British legislation passing through the House of Commons. Duffy said that while the Irish party was presenting Ireland's case at Westminister, nationalists at home should organize and use their franchise to win control over the agencies of local government. If the Irish M.P.'s were finally ejected from the House of Commons for practicing obstruction, they could return to an Ireland under nationalist domination.

[3] The idea of an independent Irish party was not new. During the Repeal agitation of 1843, an Irish Tory newspaper, the *Evening Mail,* suggested an independent Irish party to defend Irish interests and promote Irish welfare in the House of Commons. Throughout the century, Irish Con- servatives would make this suggestion when they believed British Govern- ments, Tory or Whig, were not entirely committed to Protestant Ascendancy. When things were going the way of the Protestant minority they expressed little interest in an Irish party.

Britain would eventually have to surrender to a united and disciplined national opinion controlling parliamentary representation, city corporations, poor law boards, and grand juries and capable of mobilizing effective passive resistance to British rule in Ireland.

Mitchel's recommendations were much more simple, direct, and revolutionary. He asked the Confederation to organize the country behind agitations against the payment of rents and poor rates. After a long discussion, the Confederation adopted the strategy proposed by Duffy. Repudiated by his colleagues, Mitchel resigned his offices and membership in the Confederation and began to publish a weekly newspaper, *The United Irishmen*, which advised the Irish people to prepare for revolution by collecting weapons and practicing their use. Mitchel's editorials insisted that the British must be driven out of Ireland and the Irish landlords destroyed. In an Irish Republic the land of Ireland would belong to the people of Ireland.

The February 1848, revolution in France changed the attitude of moderate Young Irelanders toward the value of physical force methods. When the news from Paris reached Dublin, they decided that the success of the French liberals indicated a possible victory for an insurrection in Ireland. Mitchel rejoined the Confederation, editorials in the *Nation* took on the same militant tone as those published in *The United Irishmen*, Smith O'Brien and his colleagues tried to enlist John O'Connell and Irish conservatives in a national front movement, contacts were made with friends of Irish freedom in the United States and Britain (the Chartists), O'Brien led a delegation to Paris to congratulate the leaders of the Second Republic and secure their support and aid for an Irish revolution, and Confederate clubs throughout the country were ordered to gather arms and prepare for war. While O'Brien was prepared to lead a rebellion against British rule in Ireland, he had no intention of making war on property. This distrust of agrarian radicalism forced Mitchel to again leave the Confederation.

In May the British Government, in an effort to frustrate a revolution before it took place, arrested O'Brien, Mitchel, and Thomas Meagher, one of the brilliant young orators of the Young Ireland movement. Juries could not agree that O'Brien and Meagher were guilty of sedition so they were released, but a packed jury convicted Mitchel of treason felony and sentenced him to transportation for fourteen years. Meanwhile, plans for revolution made little progress. Confederation leaders failed to win the cooperation of John O'Connell or the leaders of Protestant Ireland; the Catholic clergy remained hostile to Young Ireland; French Republicans, anxious to win British acceptance of their new government, refused military aid to Irish nationalists; and Irish peasants, demoralized by hunger, disease, emigration, and the split in Irish nationalism, did not have the means or the will to fight.

In July, however, the arrest of Duffy, the Government's seizure of the *Nation* offices, and the suspension of habeus corpus pushed Young Ireland into a revolution. They had neither the materials nor the leadership for success. O'Brien was a sincere patriot and a brave man, but he lacked the ruthlessness necessary in a successful revolutionary and was much too concerned with the rights of property to lead a peasant insurrection against the landlord establishment. The few peasants who answered the summons to war came with pikes to fight policemen and soldiers armed with rifles. This small, hungry, poorly equipped army, led by intellectuals full of zeal but without military experience, was easily routed in a few small engagements.

By midsummer of 1848, Irish nationalism was in shambles. Some of the Young Irelanders were in prison waiting trials that would end in sentences of transportation. Others were on the run, looking for means of escape to the United States.

In a time of crisis Young Ireland had been rejected by the priests and the people, then defeated by the British army. But Young Ireland only lost a battle. In the long run, the Young Ireland message of cultural nationalism captured the minds of the future generations of Irish nationalists. The failures of 1848 became the heroes for Fenians, Home Rulers, Gaelic Leaguers, and Sinn Feiners.[4]

After the 1848 fiasco Charles Gavan Duffy was the only prominent Young Irelander left in Ireland. He had been prosecuted five times by the Government, but brilliant defense tactics by his attorney Isaac Butt and the inability of juries to reach a unanimous decision enabled him to avoid transportation or exile. After his release from prison he revived the *Nation*, and with new allies, Dr. John Gray, a Protestant who was part owner of the leading nationalist daily newspaper *The Freeman's Journal*, and Frederick

---

[4] My views on Young Ireland expressed in this book were influenced by reading an as yet unpublished manuscript by Helen F. Mulvey, "The Young Ireland Nationalist Movement, 1842-1848."

The Young Irelanders were the most talented group ever to serve the interests of Ireland. Many of them demonstrated their abilities after 1848. Thomas D'Arcy McGee was influential in creating the federated Dominion of Canada and served as a minister in its cabinet. Duffy became Prime Minister of Victoria. Thomas Francis Meagher was a brigadier general in the Union army in the American Civil War and was appointed governor of the Montana territory. John Blake Dillon returned from exile in the United States to play a prominent role in the Irish politics of the 1860's. John Martin, Mitchel's brother-in-law, helped create the Irish Home Rule movement and the Irish parliamentary party in the 1870's. Other Young Irelanders organized the Irish Republican Brotherhood in the United States and Ireland. John Mitchel, as a journalist in the United States, fought abolition and defended the Confederate cause in the Civil War. In the 1870's he was twice elected M.P. for Tipperary, but was denied his seat because he had been convicted as a felon. Mitchel was one of the Irish examples to illustrate the ideological conflict between Liberalism and cultural nationalism: a conflict made obvious on the Continent, particularly in Germany, following 1848. Most Irish nationalists managed to harmonize Liberalism and nationalism, but Mitchel did not. His activities in the United States in defense of slavery indicated that while he was a champion of national rights he had an inadequate appreciation of individual freedom or dignity. He presents a remarkable contrast to the cosmopolitan O'Connell, who attacked slavery and insisted on the basic equality of all men.

Lucas, owner and editor of the *Tablet*, a Catholic weekly, he set out to combine the program of Lalor and Mitchel with the strategy he recommended to the Irish Confederation into a new movement to forward the interests of Ireland.

The three journalists promoted the organization of an independent Irish party in the British House of Commons —a party dedicated to the issue of tenant rights. They believed that an agitation which concentrated on the needs of farmers in all sections of the country would unite the Protestant tenant farmers of Ulster in common cause with the Catholic masses of Ulster, Leinster, Munster, and Connacht. Once there was a successful precedent of Catholic-Protestant cooperation, the old barriers of suspicion and animosity would break down, clearing the way for an Irish nationalist movement including both Catholic and Protestant opinion and energy.

Encouraged by Duffy, Lucas, and Gray, representatives of tenant societies from all four Irish provinces began to discuss common goals and methods of reaching them. These discussions produced the Irish Tenant League with the following aims: fair rents established by impartial evaluations, secure tenures for farmers who paid their rents, and the right of tenants to sell their interests in the farms they occupied. The existence of the Irish Tenant League encouraged a number of Irish M.P.'s to unite in an independent Irish party. They promised their constituents that they would remain aloof from British parties in the House of Commons and would not support any Government unwilling to enact a comprehensive program of tenant right. The independent Irish party reached the summit of its influence in July 1852, when a general election returned forty-eight Irish M.P.'s pledged to independent opposition and tenant right. But within a few months of this triumph the Irish party began the process of disintegration.

From the beginning there was a flaw in the structure of

the independent Irish party: it was a coalition of the Irish Tenant League and the Irish Brigade. The Brigade, called the Pope's Brass Band by its enemies, was the response of a small group of Liberal Irish M.P.'s to Lord John Russell's ecclesiastical titles bill (1851). This bill, threatening to prosecute and punish Catholic clergymen who took church titles derived from the United Kingdom, was a cheap effort by the Prime Minister to exploit the no-Popery hysteria following Pius IX's decision to create a diocesan structure for the Catholic Church in England.

Insulted by the British Liberal courtship of prejudice, George Henry Moore, M.P., father of the novelist George Moore, organized a small group of Irish M.P.'s to punish Russell by voting with the Opposition in an effort to destroy the Whig Government. The passage of the ecclesiastical titles bill so aroused Irish Catholic opinion that Moore decided to keep the Brigade in existence as an independent party. To give the party support in the constituencies, the Brigade M.P.'s in August 1851 organized the Catholic Defence Association of Great Britain and Ireland.

Dr. Gray and *The Freeman's Journal* endorsed the Brigade and the Catholic Defence Association. Duffy respected the talent and integrity of Moore, but had some doubts as to the latter quality in regard to some of the other Brigade M.P.'s. In August 1851, however, he helped William Sharman Crawford, M.P., the Ulster tenant right leader and champion of a federal contract between Britain and Ireland, complete an alliance between the Brigade and the Irish Tenant League. This arrangement seemed like a good bargain for the tenant righters. The alliance gave the League powerful parliamentary representation without commiting the nondenominational tenant right movement to the Catholic policies of the Brigade.

Shortly after the general election of 1852 two members of the independent Irish party, William Keogh and John

Sadleir, both Brigade M.P.'s, broke their pledge of independent opposition and accepted office in Lord Aberdeen's Peelite-Whig coalition Government. The apostasy of Sadleir and Keogh was condoned by Archbishop Paul Cullen of Dublin. Cullen had been rector of the Irish College in Rome and was a close friend of Pius IX. The Pope had appointed him rector of the Propaganda College in 1848. Cullen witnessed Mazzini's expulsion of Pius IX from Rome in 1848, and he rescued the Propaganda College by placing it under the protection of the United States government. In 1849 he was appointed Archbishop of Armagh and moved to Dublin in 1852. Cullen associated Young Ireland with Young Italy, considered Duffy the Irish Mazzini, and was convinced that the independent Irish party was permeated with the revolutionary and secular influences of Young Ireland. In addition, the Archbishop of Dublin was anxious to cooperate with the Aberdeen administration in an effort to win concessions for the Catholic Church, particularly in the area of education, and was happy to see two Catholics like Sadleir and Keogh in office.

Duffy was convinced that the treason of Sadleir and Keogh, and the support they received from Cullen and other bishops, destroyed the independent Irish party. By 1855 he had lost confidence in the movement he had helped create and in his ability to shape the future of Irish nationalism. He sold the *Nation* to A. M. Sullivan, a young nationalist from County Cork, and sailed to Australia where he eventually became Prime Minister of Victoria. As an old man he returned to Ireland as Sir Charles Gavan Duffy, endorsed the Home Rule movement, and gave Irish nationalism inspiration with his books on Young Ireland, Thomas Davis, and the independent Irish party.

The defection of Sadleir and Keogh and the conduct of some of the Catholic bishops did damage the independent Irish party, but there were other factors, just as important, which contributed to the demise of the Irish Tenant League and its parliamentary party. Aberdeen's Government attracted the support of Ulster tenant farmers. The rigours of the Famine brought a temporary solidarity in the ranks of Irish tenant farmers, but the decline of the Irish population, the result of death and emigration, and a series of good harvests in the early 1850's eased the economic pressures and pacified the agrarian population, especially in the North. There tenant farmers had better relations with landlords than in the other three provinces. With the horrors of the Famine fading into the background, ancient religious animosities reemerged and defeated the effort to create a united Irish opinion directed to the destruction of the manorial economic and social system.

The 1850's was also a decade of political resurgence by the landlords. With the Catholic hierarchy split on political policy and tactics, the landholders were able to construct an effective organization that returned fifty-seven Conservative Irish M.P.'s in the general election of 1859.[5]

This revival of landlord political power was aided by the independent Irish party's difficulty in finding suitable candidates. The prohibitive costs of contesting an election and then living in London without a salary while Parliament was in session made politics the vocation of wealthy Irishmen. Most Irishmen in a position to pursue a parliamentary career were landlords hostile to the economic, political, and religious interests of the peasant masses. Candidates prepared to gamble small fortunes to represent nationalist and tenant right causes could not always be depended on to keep their pledges once they were separated from their constituents by the Irish sea. Irishmen anxious to acquire status, prestige,

5 The landlords' victory in the general election of 1859 was also influenced by the pro-Italian, anti-Papal position of Russell and Palmerston. Cardinal Wiseman of Westminster and some Irish bishops encouraged Irish voters to support the Conservative leader, Derby, in the election.

and wealth were often willing to sell their services to any British Government in exchange for office.

By 1858 the independent Irish party had been reduced to an ineffectual twelve M.P.'s. A year later the party was officially dissolved, with most of the remaining members identifying themselves with the Liberal party. In the 1860's a number of Irish Liberal M.P.'s were active in the National Association which had as its goals Government financial support to Catholic schools from the elementary through the university level, disestablishment of the Protestant Church, and tenant right. George Henry Moore and John Blake Dillon put the Association together and enlisted the support of the Catholic hierarchy.

The Catholic Church in the Ireland of the 1860's was substantially different from the church of the 1840's. This difference was reflected by changes in clerical attitudes on religious and political subjects, a growing prosperity demonstrated in the building of churches, chapels, monasteries, convents, and educational institutions, and in a confident attitude.

O'Connell's use of the bishops and priests as essential agents of agitation had increased their influence over public opinion and conduct and helped create a confident, often arrogant, hierarchy and clergy. The prosperity of the Church was partially based on a slight improvement in the standard of living of the Catholic masses after the population decline following the Famine. The Famine not only reduced population by death and emigration, but also encouraged a pattern of later marriages which lessened the number of children born. Increased contributions to the Church also demonstrated the high regard in which the bishops and priests were held by the people and how important the litugy, values, and sacraments of the Catholic Church were in the lives of the laity. Of course, the Maynooth grant and the charitable bequests act, products of British legislation, also contributed to the financial security of a once poverty stricken institution.

In the 1860's the Catholic Church was a more conservative institution than it was in the 1840's. Although still closely tied to their peasant roots, the hierarchy and clergy were less inclined to agitation than the preceding generation of bishops and priests. This has to be stated in relative terms because the Catholic bishops and priests of Ireland would continue to be more politically active than the Catholic or Protestant clergy of other countries.

This relative decline in clerical radicalism may have been the result of a growing prosperity of the Church, more self-confidence by the bishops and priests, and a secure position of leadership in the Irish Catholic community. Another factor might have also contributed to a conservative trend in clerical thinking and action. With the arrival of Archbishop Cullen on the Irish scene in the 1850's, the Catholic Church in Ireland was in closer contact with the Vatican, and the Vatican in the reign of Pius IX was the most conservative capital in Europe. As relations with Rome increased and improved, Gallicanism declined and Ultramontane attitudes increased. Gallicanism, however, would continue to influence the character of Irish Catholicism.[6]

Because of his denunciation of Young Ireland and Fenianism and his hostility to Home Rule, Cullen, made a Cardinal in 1866, was and still is a villain to a large section of Irish nationalist opinion. Mr. Dedalus sarcastically referred to him "As another apple of God's eye!" in the bitter Christmas dinner conversation in Joyce's *Portrait of the Artist*. But when he worked with the National Association in the 1860's, Cullen demonstrated his concern with the economic needs of the Irish masses and showed a more flexible approach to

[6] My views on developments in the history of the Catholic Church in the nineteenth century have been shaped in conversations with Professor Emmet Larkin, University of Chicago, who is writing a multi-volume study of the subject.

politics than his reactionary friend, Pius IX. He was prepared to collaborate with Liberals to achieve reforms for Ireland, and he did endorse the principle of separation of Church and State, although he insisted on State funds for Catholic education. However, the ultramontane and antinationalist Cullen weakened the influence of the National Association by personal negotiations with British politicians and by using Cardinal Manning to exert pressure at Westminster. And the Irish Cardinal's excessive fear of Protestant proselytism and his view that the interests of Catholicism and the welfare of Ireland were inseparable made him insensitive to the important ideas, trends, and issues of the modern world.

The National Association worked closely with British Radicals and Dissenters in the Liberation Society in a common effort to disestablish the Protestant Church and to advance democracy by extending the franchise to the working class.[7] The compact between Irish Catholics in the National Association and British Protestant Radicals contributed to the passage of the second reform bill and to the Irish legislation of the first Gladstone administration. British no-Popery revitalized by the Vatican Council, agrarian outrage in Ireland, and the reluctance of Irish Catholics to help the disestablishment movement in Britain alienated further British Liberal support for Irish reform, but this ideologically incompatible Irish-Liberal alliance followed the precedent of the O'Connell-Whig compact and prepared the way for the coalition between Liberals and Home Rulers.

Although the National Association included respected representatives of national and tenant right interests and championed popular causes, it never succeeded in capturing the emotional commitment of the Irish masses. After the

[7] The Liberation Society began in 1853 as the Society for the Liberation of the Church from State Patronage and Control. Nonconformist leaders of the Society demanded disestablishment of the Church in Britain and Ireland, and they were also champions of an expanded suffrage and parliamentary reform.

failures of constitutional and parliamentary methods of agitation in the 1840's and 1850's, Irish national opinion was ready to consider the possibilities of physical force methods. The rise of Fenianism in the late 1850's was a reaction against the defeats suffered by constitutional movements, but it was also associated with the consequences of Irish emigration.

The Famine speeded up the pace of Irish emigration, and from 1845 to 1891 over three million Irishmen entered the United States, while many others crossed the Irish sea to find employment in the industrial boom towns of Britain. These Irish immigrants were not prepared psychologically or vocationally for life in an industrial society, and they became the most underprivileged element in the British and American urban communities. They did the hard and dirty work that native Englishmen and Americans were too proud or too weak to do. They built the railroads, dug the canals, mined the coal, scrubbed the floors, and washed the dishes in the homes of the rich. Anglo-Saxon Protestants in Britain and in Boston, New York, and Philadelphia despised these dirty, ignorant Irish Papists, and the British and American working classes hated them because they were cheap competition in the labor market. Rejected by the rest of the community, the Irish lived in their slum ghettos, producing a large proportion of the juvenile delinquents, petty thieves, alcoholics, and the prostitutes of the urban jungles.

Since the proletarian Irish were the worst victims of Britain's industrial revolution, they did make substantial contributions to Chartism in the first half of the nineteenth century, the unskilled labor movement of the 1880's and 1890's, and the spread of Syndicalism and the growth of the Labour party in the twentieth century, but as a group they were no more radical than the English, Scottish, or Welsh working classes. In general, Irish-Americans were more conservative in their economic and social views than the

Irish in Britain. They lived in a country with social mobility and economic opportunity. American capitalism might be vicious, but it provided the possibilities for wealth that could bring status in the American community.

The Irish in Britain and the Irish in America shared a commitment to Irish nationalism. They were Irish nationalists because they hated a Britain which they held responsible for the political oppression of Ireland and the economic system that forced them into exile. Irish-Americans made sacrifices for Irish nationalism for a more selfish reason. They were American nationalists. They loved their new home, they wanted to belong, they needed to be accepted by other Americans as equals. Many Irish-Americans believed that if Ireland were an independent nation Americans would then respect the Irish. In recent times, many American Jews have supported Israel's struggle for independence and survival for the same motive.

Irish-Americans and the Irish in Britain also found in Irish nationalism a psychological escape from the unpleasant realities of economic exploitation and slum living. The myths of Irish cultural nationalism, taught by Young Ireland, gave them pride and identity. It was consoling when faced with poverty and an inferior position in society to dream of the past glories of the Irish race and to have another people to blame for the fallen condition of Ireland and the Irish. And it was both pleasant and exciting to believe that though poor, an Irishman was really more noble, moral, and spiritual than "materialistic, inhuman, and bloodthirsty Saxons". In the case of the Irish in Britain and many of the Irish in America, nationalism instead of religion was the opiate of the people. Other Europeans turned to Socialism, Anarchism, Syndicalism, and Communism as expressions of proletarian protest; the Irish embraced nationalism.

Irishmen living in the cities of Britain and North America gave their loyalty, their money, and their lives to the Irish

Republican Brotherhood—a secret military society established in 1858 by some of the veterans of 1848 dedicated to the overthrow of British rule in Ireland and the establishment of an Irish Republic. John O'Mahony led the Republican movement in the United States, and James Stephens was its "Head Centre" in Ireland. Thousands of enthusiastic young men enlisted in Republican circles in Britain, Ireland, the United States, and Canada. Fenianism, another name for the Republican movement, also attracted the allegiance of a substantial number of Irishmen serving in the British army, and during the American Civil War many Irishmen enlisted in the Union and Confederate armies to gain military experience which they intended to use against Britain.[8] The famous 69th of New York has been described as a Fenian regiment.

Although the vast majority of Republicans in Ireland, Britain, and the United States represented the industrial and agrarian working classes, the Fenians, unlike O'Connell's Catholic and Repeal Associations, the Irish Confederation, the independent Irish party, or the National Association, consciously ignored social and economic questions. They believed that an independent, democratic Republic would

[8] The word Fenian came from the American name for the I.R.B., The Fenian Brotherhood. O'Mahony spoke Irish and was fascinated by the legends of the "Fianna". After the reorganization of the I.R.B. following the failure of the 1867 revolution, the Americans called their organization the Clan-na-Gael. During the American Civil War, most of the nationalists in Ireland were pro-Confederate for a number of reasons. Since they insisted on their right to dissolve the Union with Britain, they believed the South had a right to dissolve the American Union. Ireland was hurt economically by the war, and the amount of money sent home by the Irish in America declined. Many Irishmen resented the fact that a large number of casualties in the war were Irishmen, and they resented Union agents recruiting young men in Ireland. Most of the Fenians in the United States were pro-Union, but they were convinced that the war distracted Irish-American attention from the cause of Irish Republicanism (Irish attitudes toward the American Civil War were well analyzed in a paper by Joseph Hernon, "Irish sympathy for the Southern Confederacy," delivered at the Annual Conference of the American Committee for Irish Studies held at the University of Kansas, May 6 & 7, 1966).

be a panacea for Ireland's ills. Irish Republicans remained faithful to the early Young Ireland conception of Irish nationalism as independent of class and religious considerations.

In Ireland the I.R.B. was opposed by John Martin and William Smith O'Brien, the 1848 leaders who had returned from penal exile in Australia, and in the United States other forty-eighters like John Mitchel, Thomas Meagher, and Thomas D'Arcy McGee refused to endorse the movement (Mitchel in later years lost his antagonism to the I.R.B.). A. M. Sullivan in the *Nation* associated the Fenians with agrarian terrorist organizations like the Ribbon societies in a blanket condemnation of physical force nationalism. But the most powerful enemy of Republicanism was the Roman Catholic hierarchy led by Cullen. The bishops attacked the secret character of the I.R.B. and its revolutionary strategy. To Cullen the Fenians were dangerous secularists out to destroy throne and altar, radicals inspired by the excessively democratic and violent environment of the United States, and Irish disciples of Mazzini, Cavour, and Garibaldi. Bishop Moriarity told Catholics in his Kerry diocese that "hell wasn't hot enough or eternity long enough" to punish the Fenians.

From the original condemnation of the Fenians in 1858 until 1865, Cullen managed to keep his fellow bishops and the Irish priests hostile to Republicanism. There were of course some exceptions. Most Irish priests came from the tenant farmer class and naturally shared the grievances of their fathers and brothers. Some of them were bold enough to defy their superiors by giving both prayers and sympathy to the Republicans. In 1861, for instance, Father Patrick Lavelle, a Mayo priest, spoke at the Dublin funeral of Terence Bellew McManus after Cullen refused the exile who had died in San Francisco a religious burial. Lavelle was shielded from Cullen's wrath by Archbishop John MacHale of Tuam, who never went so far as to endorse Fenianism but remained on good terms with Republicans and accepted their charitable donations.

After Appomattox, Irish Republican leaders began to talk of rebellion in Ireland and demand that Stephens prepare his people for war. Irish-Americans who had recently commanded troops in the Civil War infiltrated Ireland and began to train Irish Fenians for combat. American pressure forced Stephens to plan a rising for 1866, but a factional dispute among the Republican leaders in the United States cut off military supplies to their colleagues in Ireland. Stephens refused to repeat the blunders of 1848. He called off the insurrection rather than have his pike equipped followers face the rifles and bayonets of British soldiers without guns of their own.

Meanwhile, the British Government had placed a spy in the offices of *The Irish People* and through him obtained incriminating documents. The authorities then shut down the Fenian newspaper and arrested its staff along with James Stephens.[9] A young Irish Republican, John Devoy, the future leader of the Clan-na-Gael in the United States, arranged Stephens' escape from prison. The Irish leader went to the United States, hoping to end the feud between O'Mahony and other Republicans and to persuade them to send guns and ammunition to Ireland. But Stephens was a difficult man, and his presence in the United States increased rather than diminished Fenian factionalism.

While Stephens was failing in his American mission, the Government took the Irish Republicans by surprise. Irish soldiers serving with the British army in Ireland were transferred to Britain, habeus corpus was suspended, and a number of Fenian leaders were arrested. In a futile gesture

---

9 Members of *The Irish People* staff arrested were Charles Kickham, the Irish novelist, O'Donovan Rossa, the most romantic of the Fenians, Thomas Clark Luby, who contributed to the writing of Irish history, and John O'Leary, who inspired Yeats.

of defiance, Republicans in Kerry started a revolution in February 1867, and their associates in Dublin, Cork, Tipperary, Limerick, and Clare followed the next month. These small Republican armies, lacking the necessary equipment for a respectable military showing, were easily routed by the British army and the Royal Irish Constabulary.

After 1865 a growing number of priests, influenced by depressed agricultural conditions and the increasing independence of Irish Republicans from American influences, began to view Fenianism in a more favorable light. Cullen feared that the clergy was becoming unmanageable on the Republican issue. When the British authorities treated Fenian prisoners with brutality and executed three of them —Larkin, Allen, and O'Brien (the Manchester Martyrs)— they encouraged the growth of strong pro-Fenian public and clerical opinion in Ireland.[10] Some bishops became active in the Amnesty Association, an organization to obtain the commutation of Fenian prison sentences. But the British Government was active at Rome. Aided by Bishop Moriarity and with the promises of benefits to the Church in Ireland, Odo Russell, the British representative, persuaded Pius IX to issue a Papal condemnation of the I.R.B.

Actually, Vatican interference in Irish politics on the British side antagonized Irish nationalists and increased pro-Fenian sentiment. In an effort to exploit a more friendly climate of opinion and to increase efficiency, Republicans deposed Stephens and O'Mahony and reorganized the movement on both sides of the Atlantic. But by 1870 Republicanism was in a temporary retreat from the Irish stage, and another form of constitutional nationalism, Home Rule, was waiting in the wings.

[10] Colonels T. J. Kelly and Michael Deasy, Irish-American Fenians, were rescued from a prison van in Manchester in September 1867. A policeman was killed during the escape. Allen, O'Brien, and Larkin were tried and executed for the slaying, but they were not given a fair hearing. They admitted to participation in the escape party but denied shooting the policeman.

Fenianism did not seriously challenge British rule in Ireland, but it made an impression on British opinions and encouraged William Ewart Gladstone, who became Liberal Prime Minister following the general election of 1868, to push forward a program of Irish reform. Like his former leader Peel, Gladstone decided that it was expedient for the British Government to destroy Irish nationalism by eliminating the grievances that antagonized Irish opinion. In 1869 the Prime Minister attempted to conciliate Irish Catholics by disestablishing the Irish Protestant Church, and the next year he pushed a land act through Parliament. The land act was a conservative effort to guarantee the security of tenant farmers by forcing their landlords to compensate them for improvements they had made and the disturbance created when they were evicted for any reason except the nonpayment of rent. Gladstone believed that the expense of eviction would force the landlord to think twice before clearing his estate. John Bright added an important clause to the land act providing for the government to loan up to two-thirds of the purchase price of a farm to those tenants who wanted to own the land they occupied.

As an instrument for tenant security, the land act was a failure. Since the act permitted landlords to evict without compensation if the tenant did not pay his rent, many landlords raised rents and then evicted when their tenants could not meet these exorbitant obligations. And the Bright Clause did not significantly increase the number of peasant proprietors; the loan terms were too high to permit many farmers to take advantage of the Government's offer. In fact, with the severe agricultural depression of the 1870's the conditions of the tenant class worsened, and there was a rapid increase in the number of Irish farmers evicted for the nonpayment of rents.

Though inadequate as a means of solving the Irish land question, the land act was a precedent making piece of legislation. It broke down some of the resistance to Government action in the area of land reform and thus smoothed the way for meaningful legislation in the early 1880's. And the Bright Clause pointed to the final solution of the land question—peasant proprietorship. Since the land act was the first major interference by Government with the traditional rights of landed property, it had major implications for the British as well as the Irish people. By expanding Government responsibility in social and economic areas, the land act was a significant step in the evolution of British Liberalism from its laissez faire start, at the beginning of the nineteenth century, to its collectivist welfare-state program of the late nineteenth and early twentieth centuries.

Gladstone's attempts to solve the Irish Question were too conservative to satisfy Irish nationalist opinion and too radical for the tastes of British Conservatives. They used the Prime Minister's Irish policy to rally no-Popery and anti-Irish prejudices against the Liberal Government. In addition, Gladstone's friendly intentions toward Ireland encouraged Catholic bishops to expect concessions to their demands for denominational education.

The Prime Minister agreed with the Irish Catholics' complaint that they were denied facilities and opportunities for higher education, but as leader of a party dependent on the votes of Nonconformists, he could hardly endow the Catholic University in Dublin. It would be imprudent and inconsistent to follow the disestablishment of the Protestant Church with the endowment of Catholic education. In 1873 Gladstone proposed a solution to the Irish university question which he believed would answer the demands of Catholics for higher education without compromising the principle of separation of Church and State in Ireland. His Irish university bill would have expanded Dublin University into a national institution with affiliated sectarian colleges. The university would have offered no lectures or examinations in subjects, such as theology, history, or moral philosophy, that could cause controversy between Catholics and Protestants, or among Protestants. The affiliated colleges, however, would have been free to offer courses and certificates in these academic areas.

Since the Catholic bishops had been fighting nondenominational higher education since the Queen's colleges controversy of the 1840's, they rejected Gladstone's bill as inadequate. They argued that the Government endowed Oxford and Cambridge, two Protestant universities, and that the disestablishment act left Trinity College, Dublin, a well endowed center of Protestant studies. Therefore, without Government subsidy the Catholic university, as an affiliated college of Dublic University, would not have the funds to attract either good students or faculty. Influenced by the bishops' criticism of the university bill, a considerable number of Irish Liberal M.P.'s voted against it in the House of Commons. The votes of the Irish M.P.'s meant the defeat of the university bill and forced Gladstone to call for a general election in January 1874. The British electorate, expanded by the reform bill of 1867 and emancipated by the ballot act of 1872, returned a Conservative majority to the House of Commons, and Benjamin Disraeli succeeded Gladstone as Prime Minister.[11] In Ireland, the contest between Liberals and Conservatives was of minor importance compared to the success of the Home Rule movement, which managed to return fifty-nine M.P.'s to the House of Commons.

11 All through the nineteenth century Irish and British Radicals had fought for the secret ballot. O'Connell made the secret ballot part of the platforms of the Catholic and Repeal Associations. Conditions in Ireland contributed to the passage of the secret ballot as they influenced so many important changes in the British Constitution. In 1870, 1871, and 1872 there were a number of hotly contested by-election in Ireland associated with the Home Rule cause. In these elections, priests and nationalists fought landlords, and nationalists fought priests. The violence and intimidation associated with the Irish by-elections convinced many British M.P.'s of the necessity of the secret ballot.

CHAPTER FOUR

Home Rule, 1870-1880

Isaac Butt, the father of the Home Rule movement, was born in 1813. His father was a Church of Ireland vicar in a Donegal parish. As a brilliant student at Trinity College, Butt helped found and for a time served as editor of the *Dublin University Magazine*, the most important Conservative periodical published in nineteenth-century Ireland. Butt received his degree in 1836, but stayed at Trinity to teach Political Economy. At the same time he was studying law at the King's Inn. In 1838 Butt resigned his academic position to practice as a barrister in Dublin. He started his legal career as the most prominent champion of Tory, Protestant Ascendancy, no-Popery causes. Butt argued against Irish municipal reform before the House of Lords. His unsuccessful effort to block the bill was brilliant enough to impress British and Irish Tory leaders. He was one of the few Protestants elected to the reformed Dublin Corporation. Butt confronted O'Connell in the famous Dublin Corporation Repeal debate of 1843.

Butt's defense of Tory positions, the Union, and Protestant Ascendancy was more than narrow self-interest. He viewed himself as a constructive Burkean Conservative and as an Irish patriot. The Union provided Ireland with an enlightened Constitution which protected property and political rights, and the union of Church and State guaranteed that religious values would guide political and ordinary conduct. Butt was also convinced that the Union promised peace and stability, necessary conditions for the advance of the Irish economy and a rise in the Irish standard of living.

Since Butt was raised and educated within the narrow confines of the Protestant Ascendancy, he naturally shared his coreligionists' apprehensions concerning the ambitions of Catholic nationalism. But his antagonism to Popery was more than a conditioned reflex. He believed that the Catholic masses were a superstitious, passionate, radical, and seditious rabble threatening the Union, social order, enlightened religion, property rights, and cultural values. His view of Conservatism and his brand of Irish patriotism motivated him to resist the advance of chaos and anarchy.

The evolution of Isaac Butt from the champion of Tory no-Popery to the commander of Irish nationalism actually began when he was lecturing on political economy at Trinity. He opposed the laissez faire dogmas of classical economics and insisted that the British Government had a responsibility to the impoverished masses of Ireland. His Conservative commitment made him reluctant to suggest changes in the system of landholding as necessary for general Irish prosperity; instead, he recommended tariffs to protect Irish industry and agriculture. Butt's conviction that Ireland's economic interests were independent of Britain's exposed a conditional acceptance of the Union and a smoldering economic nationalism.

By the late 1840's Butt came to realize that it was the system of Protestant Ascendancy, with its exploitation of the Catholic majority, that posed the major threat to social stability and conservative principles of government. Protestant Ascendancy created Catholic radicalism by driving the masses and their priests into the arms of demagogues preaching radical change. Butt decided that if religious and economic benefits were extended to Catholics, without serious restrictions on the rights of property or the Established Church, the Union could be preserved. Irishmen of diverse classes and faiths could work together for the common good and the progress of their country.

During the Famine, in a pamphlet published in 1847 entitled *Famine in the Land,* Butt repeated his attack on the laissez faire policies of the British Government. He suggested a program of Government relief: public works projects to provide employment and at the same time increase the economic potential of the country, expanded transportation facilities to stimulate industrial and agricultural production, and a program of emigration to relieve the strain of over-population. Butt concluded his pamphlet by warning Englishmen that they could no longer depend on class and religious antagonisms in Ireland to preserve the Union. The Famine was teaching Ireland the value of cooperation. If unity of feeling survived the present crisis, and if British politicians persisted in ignoring the needs of Ireland, the Union would perish.

Butt defended many of the Young Irelanders in the 1848 sedition trials. In speeches to the jury he blamed British misgovernment and economic policies for the condition that produced revolution in Ireland. He insisted on the constitutional right of an Irishman to demand Repeal. The Government's response to the Famine crisis indicated that British politicians lacked the knowledge or competence to deal with Irish problems. Butt suggested that a local parliament dealing with Irish affairs might not be inconsistent with the spirit of Unionism or a danger to the Empire.[1]

From 1852 until 1865 Butt had a most undistinguished career as a Conservative M.P. His positions on Irish issues,

[1] At this time Butt asked Duffy, Smith O'Brien, and Meagher to help him win a seat in the House of Commons. Duffy and Meagher said they would support Butt if he would declare himself a Repealer. Evidently Butt was not yet ready to take such an advanced position.

however, did reveal a developing nationalism. He endorsed tenant right, pressed for extensive railroad construction in Ireland, and defended Catholicism against the attacks of no-Popery bigots. After his defeat in the general election of 1865, Butt returned to Dublin to practice law and write pamphlets on the land question and denominational education. A brief stay in debtors' prison gave him unexpected leisure to write.

In his pamphlets on the tenant right issue, Butt insisted that secure tenures at fair rents, promptly paid, was a conservative solution to the land question, one that should satisfy both landlord and tenant. He also endorsed the appeal of Catholic bishops for Government funds for Catholic elementary, secondary, and university education. Irish public opinion supported denominational education as a way to preserve Ireland from radicalism and secularism, two forces permeating Britain and threatening the spiritual values of the United Kingdom. Butt's conservative reform views led him to propose the dual establishment of Catholicism and Protestantism as the answer to the religious question in Ireland.

The Fenian insurrection in 1867 made Butt a popular personality in Ireland. At great expense and personal sacrifice he enthusiastically and eloquently defended Fenian prisoners. After the trials were concluded, he served as president of the Amnesty Association which worked for years, and with some success, to have the Republicans released from prison. This generous effort in behalf of the Fenians won Butt the respect of the Irish masses.

Before 1870 Butt had recommended reform for Ireland within the framework of the Union. By the late 1860's, however, experience and frustration had convinced him that the differences between industrial Britain and agrarian Ireland were too extreme to be reconciled in a common parliament. He feared that the secularism and social, political, and economic radicalism advancing in Britain might spread to Ireland under the Union. The radical Republicanism of the Fenian movement and the influence of demagogues over Irish opinion persuaded Butt that it was time for Irish Conservatives to take the helm of Irish nationalism and steer it on a constructive course.

On the evening of May 19, 1870, forty-nine prominent Dubliners, most of them Protestant, met at the Bilton hotel to discuss the future of Ireland. Butt promoted the meeting to exploit a shift in Irish Conservative opinion that encouraged the hope of collaboration between Catholics and Protestants in an agitation to win a legislature for Ireland. Protestant leaders, angered by the disestablishment of their church, frightened by the implications of the proposed land act, and troubled by the unhealthy condition of the Irish economy, denounced the economic, religious, and political consequences of the Union. Some of them demanded a local parliament as a permanent solution to the Irish Question.

Persuaded by Butt's eloquence and logic, the meeting unanimously adopted two resolutions: the first called on the British Government to establish an Irish parliament with complete control over Irish affairs; the second established an association to achieve the requested parliament. The Home Government Association held its first meeting at the Rotunda on September 1, 1870. It was a private organization formed to unite all classes and religions behind the demand for an Irish parliament and to create a public opinion in Britain and Ireland favorable to a federal contract between the two islands.

This contract would establish an Irish parliament of Crown, Lords, and Commons with jurisdiction over local resources and revenues. The Parliament at Westminster would retain authority over common interests: colonial affairs, foreign policy, and Imperial defense. Neither the prerogatives of the Crown nor the principles of the Constitution were to be altered by the federal arrangement. In order to attract the support of the Protestant gentry and to calm

their fears and suspicions, the Association endorsed all existing religious and property rights. No issues not directly
related to self-government could be discussed at meetings.

In his book, *Irish Federalism,* published in 1870, Butt
urged Irish and British Conservatives to believe that Home
Rule would prevent rather than encourage radical excesses
in Ireland. He predicted that when Irishmen enjoyed the
benefits of self-government they would cease rebellious
activities. They would become the most loyal supporters
of the Crown and Constitution in the Empire. Irish Catholics
were influenced by their religious training to distrust democratic and extremist ideologies. Under normal circumstances
they would follow conservative leaders. If these assurances
were inadequate to satisfy sceptics, Butt reminded his readers
that a Protestant and Conservative Irish House of Lords
would block radical proposals emanating from an Irish House
of Commons.[2]

From its beginning the Home Government Association
enjoyed successes. The Dublin Corporation, poor law boards,
town councils, tenant right organizations, and many newspapers endorsed the program of the Association. Local
branches of the Association in England and Scotland multi-
plied so rapidly that in 1873 it was found necessary to
organize the Home Rule Confederation of Great Britain,
with Butt as president.[3] And in the period extending from

[2] Butt's book on Federalism was directed at British and Irish Conservative
opinion. He knew, of course, that an Irish House of Lords could block
essential Irish reforms. Like O'Connell, Butt believed that an Irish Parliament located in Dublin would be Irish in sentiment and point of view and
would be influenced by Irish opinion. In time, even the Irish House of
Lords would submit to the mood of the country and would fulfill its
obligations to the people who looked to the aristocracy for justice, mercy,
and leadership.

[3] Many of the leaders of the Home Rule Confederation of Great Britain
were Fenians. They had much more energy and devotion to Irish nationalism than members of the Home Rule League. The main task of the Confederation was to organize the Irish vote in British cities and to use this
vote to commit British candidates for Parliament to support Home Rule
for Ireland.

January 1871 to August 1873 Irish voters in by-elections returned eight Home Rulers to the House of Commons; and six Irish Liberals already in Parliament announced their support for the principle of Federalism. These victories were balanced by the inability of the Association to win the approval of the Protestant gentry or the blessing of the Catholic hierarchy.

Butt made a special effort to enroll Protestant landlords in the Home Government Association. He told them that tenant farmers were prepared to accept their political guidance; he also warned them that this might be their last opportunity to reach a settlement with their Catholic neighbors. If Protestants fought this effort to win an Irish parliament, they could expect little respect for their religious or property interests in an independent Ireland.

Some Protestants did become Home Rulers in reaction to Gladstone's Irish policy. They fondly recalled the Irish Protestant nation of the eighteenth century and believed that Protestant rights would receive more respect in a revived Irish legislature, dominated by the gentry, than in a British Parliament controlled by Liberals. When early enthusiasm cooled to sober reflection, however, many Protestants who once had been attracted to Home Rule realized that there was a wide gap separating the ultimate objectives of the Catholic masses and their own interests. Now they were dealing with tenant farmers who could use the suffrage and the secret ballot to establish a peasant democracy. Perhaps, they decided, it would be better to rely on the protection of a British Parliament, with its strong Protestant Conservative representation, than on Catholic promises of moderation and good will. While Protestants, mostly of the middle class, continued to play an important role in the Association, few others applied for membership after the initial fervor of the spring and summer of 1870. Many of those initially enrolled ceased to take an active interest in Federalism. Irish newspapers commented on Protestant apathy concerning Home Rule. Alfred Webb, a Quaker official of the association, advised nationalists to abandon hope of "attaching any large number of our Protestant fellow countrymen."[4]

While Federalist propaganda concentrated on the Protestant gentry, Butt and his friends also realized the necessity of securing the good will of the Catholic hierarchy and clergy. By 1870, however, most of the bishops and priests were firmly attached to Gladstone's coattails. They had hopes that the Prime Minister would endow the Catholic University in Dublin and were suspicious of nationalist agitations which diverted attention from the religious education issue. When invited to join the Home Government Association, many bishops and priests said they would not participate in any movement dominated by anti-Catholic Protestants. They suggested that so-called Protestant nationalists were using Home Rule to undermine the priests' influence with the people and to attack a Liberal Government anxious to extend justice and friendship to Ireland. Because the hierarchy was cool to Home Rule, few priests applied for membership in the Home Government Association. Some prominent politicians also avoided contact with a movement frowned on by the hierarchy. On numerous occasions Home Rule candidates in by-elections encountered clerical opposition. They

---

[4] A lack of records makes it difficult to estimate the actual number of Protestants who joined the Home Government Association between 1870 and 1873. It does seem clear that only a few members of the gentry became Home Rulers and that most Protestant Federalists came from the world of trade and commerce. Almost all of the Protestant majority at the Bilton meeting were merchants, and Protestant nationalism was described by Thomas Conolly, Conservative M.P. for Donegal, as a device to put money into the pockets of Dublin businessmen. Protestant merchants were critical of Gladstone's Irish policy, but they were also disturbed by the decline in the Irish economy resulting from rents paid to absentee landlords, emigration, and the competition from British industry. In 1871, according to the *Nation*, Protestants composed two-fifths of the Home Government Association membership and had a majority of three on its sixty-one man Executive Council. In June 1872 the *Nation* reported that in the recent election for the Executive Council, Protestants cast only one-third of the ballots and Catholics had a majority of seven on the Council.

usually emerged victorious, but the bitterness of the contests did nothing to reconcile the hierarchy to Federalism.[5]

After the House of Commons rejected the Irish university bill, Home Government Association officials tried to exploit the bishops' dissatisfaction with Gladstone's solution to the Irish university question. In pronouncements condemning the university bill, several prelates did advocate Home Rule as an initial step in the direction of denominational education. A few went further by complimenting the program and leadership of the Home Government Association. This apparent softening in the hierarchy's attitude toward Federalism encouraged a number of priests to endorse the Home Rule movement.

Many Federalists interpreted the election of Home Rule candidates for Parliament and the conversion of Catholic priests to Home Rule principles as signs that the Association had succeeded in educating Irish opinion on the merits of Federalism. Now was the time, they said, to replace the Home Government Association with an organization open to public participation. Twenty-five thousand people, including twenty-five M.P.'s, signed a requisition calling for a national conference to discuss and plan the future of Home Rule.

[5] Dr. David Moriarity of Kerry told the Catholics of his diocese that some Home Rule leaders were anti-Catholic. He advised them to ignore Federalism and to place their confidence in Gladstone and the Liberals. In the Archdiocese of Dublin, dominated by the personality of Cardinal Cullen, in the period 1870-1873 only two priests joined the Home Government Association. One of them later withdrew. The names of twenty Protestant clergymen and only twelve Catholic priests appeared on a list of Home Government Association members published in the *Nation* in 1870. Some of the Catholic clergy were hostile to Butt when he successfully contested Limerick in 1871. Joseph Ronayne, another victorious Home Rule candidate in a Cork City by-election, had to run against the opposition of a number of priests. Rowland Blennerhassett, Home Ruler and Protestant landlord from Kerry, managed to win a seat in the House of Commons despite the opposition of Bishop Moriarity. Joseph Biggar, however, was defeated in Derry because the bishop, Francis Kelly, and his clergy campaigned for the Liberal candidate, split the nationalist vote, and thus guaranteed a Conservative victory.

On November 18, 1873, the national conference convened at the Rotunda in Dublin. During the four days of the meeting, nine hundred delegates approved resolutions supporting a federal contract between Britain and Ireland, insisting that nationalist M.P.'s were responsible to their constituents and future national conferences, and substituting the Home Rule League for the Home Government Association. Anyone who paid one pound in dues every year and was willing to accept the resolutions of the national conference could become a member of the Home Rule League. Later, to give Home Rule more popular support and to increase the income of the League, Butt borrowed a tactic used by O'Connell when he organized the Catholic and Repeal Associations. Anyone who contributed one shilling a year could become an associate member of the Home Rule League.

In three years Isaac Butt had done much to revitalize Irish nationalism after the failures of Repeal in the 1840's, the independent party in the 1850's, and the Fenian movement of the 1860's had caused Irishmen to lose confidence in both constitutional and physical force methods of agitation. In 1873 many Irishmen once more enjoyed the hope of an independent parliament in Dublin.

Butt's effort to convince Irish opinion that Federalism was the solution to the Irish Question was aided by the inadequacy of Gladstone's Irish legislation. When Irish farmers realized that the land act would not result in secure tenures at fair rents, and when the Catholic clergy discovered that Gladstone had no intention of conceding their education demands, they moved into the ranks of Home Rule. Although the mild platform of the Home Government Association offered no solutions to the education and agrarian questions, priests and farmers were ready to use Federalism as an outlet for their frustrations. They seemed to accept the Association's idealistic assumptions that an Irish parliament would be able to harmonize conflicting class, economic, and religious interests.

Unfortunately, the Home Government Association did not succeed in reconciling Catholic and Protestant viewpoints. When considered realistically there was little chance of resolving religious differences in the Ireland of the 1870's. Protestants were still too suspicious of the motives of Catholic nationalists to abandon their parochialism and their dependence on the British Parliament for protection in what they considered a hostile environment. Perhaps if the land act had proved more successful in increasing the security of tenant farmers, or if the Catholic hierarchy had not been so determined to win Government financial support for their schools, a Catholic-Protestant nationalist alliance might have resulted. But without the land and education issues Home Rule could never have enlisted the support of the Catholic priests and people. And it was far more important for a nationalist agitation to have the encouragement of the Catholic majority than the allegiance of the Protestant minority.

❖   ❖   ❖   ❖

Isaac Butt reached the high point of his nationalist career when Irish voters elected fifty-nine Home Rule M.P.'s in 1874. Shortly after the general election, the nationalist M.P.'s met in Dublin and organized the Irish Home Rule parliamentary party, with Butt as chairman.

The rules of conduct, the objectives, and the parliamentary strategy of the Irish party reflected Butt's conservative approach to politics. Home Rule M.P.'s had to vote as a unit only on the issue of self-government. On other questions they were permitted to act as their consciences and interests dictated. Butt rejected Charles Gavan Duffy's concept of a completely independent, strongly disciplined Irish party, voting as a block on all legislation touching Irish interests. He said that members of his party were not of one opinion on British, Imperial, or even Irish questions. Independent opposition would create the impression that the Irish were allied with the Liberals against the Conservatives. Tight discipline would force the party to have definite positions on the land and religious questions and would convince Irish Protestants that Irish nationalism could not be divorced from Catholicism and agrarian radicalism.

Butt knew that by appeasing the gentry he risked alienating the Catholic masses. He tried to compensate by urging Home Rule M.P.'s as individuals, not as Irish party members, to support his efforts to amend the land act, reform the Irish suffrage, and win a system of denominational education for Ireland. The plan was too complex to work. How many nationalist or Unionist voters would make the effort to distinguish between the individual actions of Home Rule M.P.'s and the public image of the Irish party?

The parliamentary strategy of the Irish party can best be described as a policy of conciliation. Butt was convinced that the conservative principles underlying Federalism, and the good manners and courtesy of Irish nationalist M.P.'s, would finally persuade British M.P.'s to consider the case for Home Rule with an open mind. He instructed his colleagues to conduct themselves as gentlemen in the House of Commons, always respecting parliamentary traditions and procedures. He also advised them to display their loyalty to the Crown, their willingness to share the burdens of Empire, and their admiration for the principles of the British Constitution.

Victory in the general election of 1874 and the formation of the Irish party created much optimism in Irish nationalist circles. By 1876, however, after three years of defeat and disappointment in the House of Commons, cynicism had replaced optimism, and the Irish party was considered by many as just another group of opportunists exploiting nationalism to improve their own prospects. The failure of the Irish party to satisfy the hopes of 1874 can be attributed to the unsatisfactory quality of its members, Butt's inadequacies as a leader, and the miscalculations of his parliamentary strategy.

Like the Repeal party of the 1830's and 1840's and the independent Irish party of the 1850's, the Irish parliamentary party of the 1870's suffered from the less than mediocre talent of its parliamentary representation. As pointed out in the previous chapter, financing an election campaign and providing for maintenance in London during a parliamentary session was beyond the means of most sincere nationalists. This left the political field to men often long on cash but short on integrity and talent. The short interval between the national conference and the general election made it impossible for the newly formed Home Rule League to exert much influence in the selection of candidates. Consequently, the constituencies in 1874 had no choice but to accept politicians who in many cases adopted Federalism only to retain or obtain seats in the House of Commons. Once elected, these men neglected their parliamentary duties and made light of their commitment to Home Rule. Absenteeism from the House of Commons by half-hearted Home Rule M.P.'s was directly responsible for the defeat of two Irish franchise reform bills and weakened the party showing in other important tests of strength.

The apathy of Home Rule M.P.'s was encouraged by Butt's deficiencies as a party leader. He was a skilled debater, brilliant in framing legislation, and personally popular with British politicians; but these assets were balanced by a timidity in combat, a reluctance to enforce party discipline, and financial problems that made it difficult for him to concentrate on his duties as party chairman. His financial difficulties necessitated frequent absences from the House of Commons, often at times when his ability and experience were needed.

When put to the test, Butt's policy of conciliation was a failure. British politicians were not impressed with the logic behind Federalism and considered it just another Irish attempt to destroy the Union and disrupt the Empire. The freedom of action permitted Irish party M.P.'s was unsatisfactory to all shades of Irish opinion. Members of the Ascendancy remained convinced that Catholicism, agrarian radicalism, and nationalism were an inseparable trinity. Most Irish Catholics insisted that tenant right and religious education were intrinsic to the objectives of nationalism. They found it difficult to give their enthusiasm to a movement which divorced political from social, economic, and religious grievances.

The criticisms of the Home Rule M.P.'s and the Irish party, which began during the parliamentary session of 1874, were widespread when Parliament adjourned in 1876. Tenant right leaders and denominational education advocates accused Home Rule M.P.'s of insincerity in pressing their grievances. Some of them suggested the abandonment of Federalism for an agitation more sympathetic to Catholic and agrarian interests. T. D. Sullivan, editor of the *Nation* while his brother A. M. held a seat in the House of Commons, was critical of the Irish party's conciliatory parliamentary policy. He advised Home Rulers to employ obstruction in the House of Commons. Obstruction would be a proper response to the indifference British politicians displayed toward Irish issues. Sullivan's suggestion was a major topic of newspaper debate in the summer of 1876. Most nationalist newspapers expressed a preference for obstruction over conciliation.

During the annual convention of the Home Rule Confederation of Great Britain, held in Dublin in August 1876, delegates criticized the apathetic performances of Home Rule M.P.'s and the parliamentary tactics of the Irish party. They passed a resolution expressing loyalty to Butt as leader, but also insisting on more discipline in the Irish party and a dynamic parliamentary policy. Butt assented to the resolution, committing himself and the party to a more resolute course of action in the House of Commons. This promise was given under duress, and Butt, by his subsequent conduct at Westminister, indicated that he had no intention of carrying it out.

In 1877 the obstructive tactics used by Charles Stewart Parnell and Joseph Biggar diverted the attention of Irish nationalists from the actions of other Home Rule M.P.'s. Parnell, a Protestant landlord from County Wicklow, was elected Home Rule M.P. for Meath in 1875. During his first two years in the House of Commons Parnell seldom spoke, but was always present for debates and divisions. He was impressed with Joseph Biggar's experiment with obstruction during the parliamentary session of 1875. Biggar delayed passage of an Irish coercion bill by reading long passages from parliamentary blue books. Biggar's use of obstruction outraged Butt, who always insisted that Home Rulers should act like gentlemen and play by the accepted rules of Parliament.

Joseph Biggar was a Protestant provision merchant from Belfast. He joined the Irish Republican Brotherhood and became a member of its Supreme Council. The I.R.B. expelled him in 1877 because of his Home Rule loyalties. Biggar was an early member of the Home Government Association and was elected a Home Rule M.P. for Cavan in the general election of 1874.

During the parliamentary session of 1877 Parnell and Biggar, supported by a handful of their colleagues, impeded the Government's legislative programs with motions to adjourn or to report progress and with amendments to almost every bill on the docket. Some of the amendments were quite constructive, but they necessitated long discussions that seriously delayed the Government's timetable.

British newspapers and periodicals attacked Parnell and Biggar as uncouth Irish ruffians. Butt described their parliamentary conduct as insubordination threatening the existence of the Irish party. He condemned obstruction as a negative policy that would intensify anti-Irish sentiment in Britain and encourage a conviction that Irishmen were incompetent to govern themselves.

Parnell and Biggar denied that their consistent attendance in the House of Commons, frequent motions, and numerous amendments constituted an attempt to paralyze the machinery of government. They described their efforts as a method to insure adequate discussion of legislation at times convenient for M.P.'s to be present. Parnell argued that if conscientious devotion to duty by members of the House of Commons delayed the parliamentary schedule, this was a good argument in support of the Home Rule position that the British Parliament should share her complex burdens with subordinate legislatures.

In defending his parliamentary tactics Parnell ridiculed Butt's thesis that reason could persuade British politicians to concede reform and self-government to Ireland. He said that Liberals and Conservatives seldom took the time to listen to Irish claims, no matter how well they were argued. All that really counted in the House of Commons was party strength, and the Irish party .was weak in numbers and morale. Parnell insisted that Ireland could achieve Home Rule only with the support of one of the British political parties. To get this support, Home Rule M.P.'s must use intimidation rather than reason. They must make their presence felt in the House of Commons by constant attention to duty and by bringing their influence to bear on issues that directly touched Britain and the Empire. They must present Parliament with a clear choice: Home Rule for Ireland or persistent Irish interference in British and Imperial affairs. Parnell said that if this active parliamentary policy failed to achieve self-government, then the Irish people might as well abandon all confidence in constitutional methods of agitation.

Obstruction or conciliation? That was the issue debated by Butt, Parnell, and their partisans in newspapers, nationalist organizations, meetings of the Irish party, tenant right societies, and on political platforms in Ireland and Britain. Butt fought with unusual energy though with little effect. Slowly but surely, Parnell collected the support of national opinion. Newspapers praised the man who dared to defy the House of Commons and recommended his parliamentary policy to other Home Rule M.P.'s. A growing number of Butt's friends in the Irish party advised him to compromise his quarrel with Parnell by adopting a more vigorous parliamentary policy. For the most part, it was the despised absentee and Whig elements in the party that remained uncompromisingly loyal to Butt. The Home Rule Confederation of Great Britain was pro-Parnell. In 1877 the Irish in Britain refused to re-elect Butt as the president of their organization and replaced him with Parnell. Supporters of Parnell forced the Home Rule League to call another national conference to decide the question of parliamentary policy. The conference, held in January 1878, voted to retain Butt as leader of the Irish party, but instructed him to lead a united party with a dynamic parliamentary policy.

When Butt organized the Home Rule movement, a number of Fenians in Ireland and Britain joined the Home Government Association, the Home Rule League, or the Home Rule Confederation of Great Britain. Across the Atlantic, American Fenians rejected Home Rule because it involved constitutional and parliamentary methods of agitation. But the work of Parnell and Biggar in the House of Commons suggested to the leaders of the Clan-na-Gael that a parliamentary party led by a man of Parnell's qualities, using obstruction as a weapon, might achieve results for Irish nationalism.

Leaders of the Clan-na-Gael were anxious to reach an understanding with Parnell so that they could complete plans for a "New Departure" in Irish nationalism. Irish-Americans

like John Devoy and John Boyle O'Reilly were convinced
that Britain would become involved in the Russo-Turkish
war on the side of the Turks. They believed that Ireland
could exploit Britain's preoccupation with a war in the
Balkans to extort concessions to Irish nationalism. They
hoped to repeat the victory of 1782 when Britain, on the
defensive in a war against France, submitted to armed Ireland's demand for an extension of the liberties of the Irish
Parliament. The Fenians, however, were in no position to
suggest policy to the Irish people. Too many years of subter-
ranean activity had cut them off from the mainstream of
Irish affairs.

The "New Departure" was a two point program for
bridging the gap separating the Irish masses from the Republican movement. Devoy and his colleagues decided to
support an agitation for peasant proprietorship as a stratagem
to arouse national enthusiasm among the politically apathetic
peasantry suffering from the agricultural depression that
struck the British Isles in the 1870's. Republican endorsement of agrarian radicalism would not only attract peasant
enthusiasm, but it might also lead to an alliance with those
Home Rule M.P.'s still enjoying the confidence of the public.
According to the "New Departure" blueprint, freedom would
be achieved when the peasant masses became ardent nationalists and a significant number of Home Rule M.P.'s committed themselves to complete separation from Britain. When
that time came, the M.P.'s would initiate the struggle for
independence by withdrawing from the British Parliament
and by establishing a provisional Irish government in Dublin.
All Ireland would stand ready to support the provisional
government with arms supplied by Fenians in the United
States.

In October 1878 the Republicans in the United States
offered Parnell specific terms for an alliance. These terms
included "abandonment of the federal demand and substitu-

tion of a general declaration in favor of self-government";
vigorous agitation of the land question on the basis of peasant
proprietorship, while accepting concessions to abolish arbitrary eviction; an Irish party united on all Irish and Imperial
questions pursuing an aggressive parliamentary policy; and
"advocacy of all struggling nationalities in the British Empire
and elsewhere."

Parnell, while not as interested in or as sympathetic to the
problems of the tenant farmers as Butt, realized the value
of combining the agrarian and nationalist agitations and
understood the importance of Irish-American financial support, but he was reluctant to conclude a compact with the
Republicans on their own terms. Such an agreement might
influence some members of the Catholic hierarchy to oppose
his bid to control the Home Rule movement. While waiting
for a favorable opportunity to come to terms with Irish-
Americans, Parnell and his colleagues in the active wing of
the Irish party joined forces with agrarian radicals. During
the fall of 1878 they spoke to a number of tenant right meetings. At one of them, John O'Connor Power, M. P. for Mayo,
proclaimed the future slogan of the Land League: "the land
of Ireland for the people of Ireland."

Although a compact between Parnell and the Irish-American Republicans was not completed until 1879, Butt was
convinced that an alliance already existed to destroy the
constitutional movement. In the autumn of 1878 he made a
final effort to preserve conservative nationalism. He ad-
dressed a manifesto to the Irish people warning them that
obstruction would lead to the expulsion of Irish M.P.'s from
the House of Commons, the disfranchisement of nationalist
voters, the resurgence of physical force nationalism, and,
inevitably, bloody defeat on the battlefield.

Few people heeded Butt's warning. His parliamentary
activities in 1878 completely discredited him with Irish
national opinion. In exchange for an intermediate education

bill which created government scholarships for students in Catholic secondary schools, Butt promised to support the Conservative Government's foreign and Imperial policy. True to his bargain, and consistent with his pro-imperialistic personal convictions, Butt defended Disraeli's actions at the Congress of Berlin against Liberal criticism. When Parliament convened in December 1878 to deal with the crisis in Afghanistan, he blocked the efforts of other Home Rule M.P.'s to submit an amendment to the Queen's Speech asking for a redress of grievances. Butt said that the amendment would embarrass the Government during a period of international tension. He insisted that Home Rulers should be patriotic supporters of Crown and Empire.

Nationalist newspapers were dumbfounded that the champion of Irish Home Rule would defend and support the Imperialism of a Tory Government. Even Butt's warmest newspaper supporters, those who sided with him against Parnell in the controversy over obstruction, disowned him for encouraging "a government avowedly hostile to the claims of Ireland."

In this atmosphere of suspicion, disillusionment, and controversy, the annual meeting of the Home Rule League took place in Dublin on February 4, 1879. T. D. Sullivan gave notice of two resolutions he intended to submit for League approval. The first was a vote of censure on Butt for violating the party pledge of 1874 by personally negotiating with the Government on the education question; the second demanded increased activity and consistent attendance in the House of Commons from Home Rule M.P.'s. Butt persuaded Sullivan to withdraw his censure motion, but he suffered a defeat when the second resolution passed by a margin of eight votes. This was the end for Isaac Butt. He left the meeting on the arm of his son. Death spared him further humiliation. A few weeks after the League meeting he became ill, never recovered, and died of a stroke on May 5, 1879.

William Shaw, M.P. for Cork, a Nonconformist clergyman and a successful banker, was elected to replace Butt as Irish party chairman. Under his direction the party failed to improve its undistinguished performance in the House of Commons. Meanwhile, Parnell was preparing to test his strength at the next general election. In October 1879 he helped Michael Davitt launch the National Land League. Davitt was a released Fenian prisoner who had gone to the United States and become a convert to the principles of the "New Departure". He returned to Ireland to lead the agrarian phase of the new strategy.

From January to March 1880 Parnell was in the United States completing an alliance with the Clan-na-Gael, on his terms, and soliciting funds from Irish-Americans for the "New Departure". Parnell returned from his triumphant American tour just in time for the March general election. He personally contested and won three seats. When all the returns were in, Irish voters had elected sixty-one Home Rule M.P.'s, most of them supporters of Parnell. On April 26, 1880, the Irish parliamentary party met and held its election for chairman. Parnell defeated Shaw by twenty-three votes to eighteen. Thus ended the era of Butt's conciliation policy and commenced the vigorous ten year reign of Charles Stewart Parnell over the forces of Irish nationalism.[6]

❀   ❀   ❀   ❀

Although the Home Rule movement under Butt's leadership failed to achieve significant victories, the period 1870-1880 was more than just a false start or a prelude to a more

[6] Shaw and about twenty of his supporters could not accept Parnell's leadership and sat as independent nationalists working with the Liberal party. Most of them were replaced by Parnellites in the general election of 1885. In the 1880's Parnell lost the support of two former "obstructionist" colleagues, John O'Connor Power and F. Hugh O'Donnell. There is reason to believe they were jealous of Parnell and thought themselves more qualified for leadership.

glorious era of nationalism. Despite his weakness of character, his gentleness, his limited view of independent opposition, and his naive respect for the British political tradition, Butt made a major contribution to the development of Irish nationalism. He articulated the Home Rule demand, created a public opinion to support it, and organized an Irish party to win it in the British Parliament. For all of its many weaknesses and failures, the Irish party in the 1870's was in quality and quantity the best representation Irish nationalism had had in the British Parliament. Home Rule M.P.'s publicized Irish grievances, introduced reform measures, and, in some instances, interested British Liberals in Irish causes.

If successful, Butt's brand of Federalism would have put an end to those class and religious hatreds dividing the Irish community; it would also have eased the centuries-old tensions that warped Anglo-Irish relations. Unfortunately, Butt's political realism did not match his good intentions. Irish Protestants could not cooperate in a nationalist movement with Catholics. They were dominated by a hysterical fear that an Irish Parliament would be controlled by a Catholic peasant democracy lusting after the spoils of Protestant property and political influence. Distrust of Catholics and faithfulness to class and property interests combined to create a separate Irish Protestant nationalism committed to the British connection. On the other hand, after experiencing centuries of exploitation, Catholic tenant farmers could not have confidence in Protestant landlord nationalism.

The British Parliament rejected Butt's arguments for Home Rule for the same reason that it had rejected O'Connell's demands for Repeal. To British parliamentary and public opinion, Irish independence, no matter how restricted, was a knife pointed at the heart of the concept of the British Empire, a repudiation of traditional property interests, and a Catholic tactic to establish religious ascendancy in Ireland. Butt was bucking a tide of imperialism. Imperialism had become a badge of identity for the Conservative party, and Conservatives had used it to attract the allegiance of British voters.

Though less intellectual than Butt and lacking his parliamentary experience, Parnell had better insights into the true character of British politics in the 1870's. He realized that Irish Protestants as a group would not embrace Home Rule and that nationalism must be grounded on the enthusiasm of the Catholic masses and the dollars of Irish-Americans. Parnell observed that British M.P.'s were not swayed by logical arguments in the House of Commons. They voted in conformity to British interests and party discipline. Before making concessions to Irish nationalism they must be convinced that such concessions served the interest of Britain and their political parties. In order to impress British politicians with its determination and to compensate for its lack of numbers Parnell decided that the Irish party must have tight discipline. It had to retaliate for British indifference to Irish concerns with systematic sabotage of vital British and Imperial legislation. This determination would make British leaders realize the potential danger of Irish discontent and force them to offer concessions to Irish nationalism. Parnell's parliamentary strategy was based on a simple but effective formula: if the British Parliament denied freedom and reform to the Irish people, the Irish party would deny the British people effective government.

Obstruction, however, was even more important as a tactic to capture the enthusiasm of the Irish masses. To sustain this enthusiasm and to obtain financial support Parnell endorsed the program of agrarian radicals and negotiated an alliance with Irish-Americans. Eventually this alliance between the parliamentary party, tenant righters, and Irish-Americans would achieve security of tenures at fair rents and finally peasant proprietorship for Irish farmers. It would win an expanded suffrage, increased authority in local government, and enlarged educational opportunities for residents of Ireland. It would also extract commitment to Home Rule from the Liberal party. Parnell and the Home Rule movement he revived and modified would come as close to achieving the Irish hope of freedom as constitutional methods permitted.

CHAPTER FIVE

Home Rule, 1880-1906

When Parnell took control of the Irish party he was, as president of the National Land League, commanding an agrarian agitation that bordered on revolution. The Land League was generously endowed with Irish-American money and in March 1880 had a balance of over 20,000 pounds. Peasant proprietorship was the League's solution to the land question, but it was prepared to advance to its ultimate goal in stages. In the late 1870's and early 1880's Land Leaguers demanded secure tenures at fair rents and advised tenant farmers to hang on to their farms, to refuse to pay excess rents or to occupy the farms of evicted members of their own class, and to boycott rack-renting landlords and those tenant farmers who cooperated with the system of landlordism.[1] The League used its financial resources to help the victims of eviction, and this support raised the morale of tenant farmers.

Irish landlords, British politicians, and Conservative journalists described the Land League campaign as a revolutionary class war against the rights of property and Ireland as a country in a state of anarchy. The Royal Irish Constabulary, a para-military police force, and sometimes even soldiers, had to be used to evict stubborn tenants from their farms and, in the war against landlordism, militant tenant farmers burned the hayricks of unpopular landlords and maimed their cattle. Agents of offending landlords, and tenant farmers who rented farms of evicted friends of the Land League, were boycotted and sometimes suffered physical reprisals.

Following the Liberal victory in the general election of 1880, Gladstone returned as Prime Minister. The militancy of the Land League and the turbulence in Ireland convinced him that he must attempt another effort at Irish reform. Gladstone introduced a bill to compensate evicted tenants, but it was defeated in the House of Lords. Increased agitation pushed the Prime Minister further in the direction of tenant right. In 1881 he employed coercion in an attempt to halt violence, but he also introduced a land bill providing for fixity of tenure at fair rents and for free sale of the tenant's interest in the farm. With the Queen's influence, this bill passed through the House of Lords in late August 1881. In addition to establishing dual ownership of the Irish land, and clearing the way for peasant proprietorship, the land act was a devastating blow to the remnants of laissez faire economic dogmas. And the enemies of the act pointed out that this emergency legislation for Ireland established dangerous precedents for Britain.

1 In a speech delivered on September 19, 1880, at Ennis, County Clare, Parnell told Irish tenant farmers to hang on to their farms and to refuse to pay unjust rents. If they were evicted and someone bid for their farms, they should not resort to violence in revenge. "I wish to point out to you a very much better way—a more Christian and charitable way, which will give the lost man an opportunity of repenting. When a man takes a farm from which another has been evicted, you must shun him on the roadside when you meet him—you must shun him in the streets of the town—you must shun him in the shop—you must shun him on the fair-green and in the market place, and even in the place of worship, by leaving him alone, by putting him in a moral Coventry, by isolating him from the rest of the country, as if he were the leper of old—you must show him your detestation of the crime he has committed. . ." This policy of the rent strike, accompanied by shunning the supporters of landlordism, was developed into an effective policy and first applied to an estate in County Mayo where Captain Boycott was agent. Boycott became the name for the new tactic.

Parnell did not accept Gladstone's major concession to Irish agitation with any demonstration of gratitude. Instead, he rejected the bill as inadequate because it did not cover those tenants already in arrears. But the main reason Parnell did not support the land act on its second reading involved tactics. He did not want to be responsible for a bill that might prove to have flaws in its execution, and he wanted to be free to press for amendments and further land reform. To Parnell, the land agitation was an instrument to mold a militant national opinion. The leader of nationalist Ireland must never accept any British concession as completely satisfactory. He must always push for more until Home Rule was achieved.

After the land act was law, Parnell continued the agrarian agitation in his effort to force further reform legislation and to influence the rent fixing tribunals to keep the obligations of the tenant farmer as low as possible. Finally Gladstone lost patience and used the provisions of the coercion bill to place Parnell and a few of his lieutenants in Kilmainham Gaol, Dublin. Parnell retaliated by issuing a no-rent manifesto, which had little effect since it was opposed by influential members of the Catholic hierarchy and clergy. But imprisonment increased Parnell's stature as a nationalist leader and encouraged rather than retarded violence in rural Ireland. So in April 1882 the Government commenced negotiations with the Home Rule leader which culminated in the Kilmainham Treaty. Gladstone promised to settle the arrears question and to suspend coercion; Parnell agreed to issue a public statement accepting the land act as "a practical settlement of the land question" and to collaborate with the Liberals in efforts to forward Irish reform. Parnell and his associates were released from prison on May 2, 1882.

Parnell had used agrarian radicalism to mobilize the Irish masses, but now it was time to consolidate the unruly forces he led, discipline the national movement, and push the demand for Home Rule. In 1882 the Irish National League and the Irish National League of Great Britain replaced the Home Rule League and the Home Rule Confederation of Great Britain. The local branches of the Irish National League sent delegates to county and city conventions to meet with representatives of the Catholic clergy. Together they selected Home Rule candidates for general and by-elections. The branches and the conventions gave a democratic image and spirit to the Home Rule movement, but the Irish parliamentary party controlled the selection of candidates. Home Rule M.P.'s chaired the sessions of the conventions and usually persuaded delegates to accept the candidates desired by the party. Home Rule M.P.'s residing in London dominated the Irish National League of Great Britain. They used the organization to mobilize the Irish vote in British cities to serve the interests of Irish nationalism.

The Land League was outlawed in 1881, and Parnell was content to see it go. Too many Fenians antagonistic to parliamentary methods and the Home Rule movement were influential in the League. They lessened Parnell's control over the agrarian agitation and kept the League from fully cooperating with the Irish party.[2] Parnell took over the funds of the Land League and used the money, along with the contributions that still were collected from Irish-American and Irish sources, to contest general and by-elections.[3] Now the nationalist movement no longer had to depend on opportunists. With such financial support the Irish party could select dedicated and talented young men from all classes of society, pay their election expenses, and, if neces-

[2] In October 1881, while Parnell was in prison, the Land League was outlawed. The Ladies Land League, under the presidency of Parnell's sister, carried on the agitation. Parnell liquidated the Ladies Land League in 1882 as an obstacle to nationalist unity.

[3] After the demise of the Land League, Irish-American contributions to the nationalist cause radically declined. But in the general election of 1885 Irish-Americans once more began to contribute generously to the Home Rule movement.

sary, provide them with a salary while they served their country at Westminister. An efficient election machine, money, and household suffrage (the product of the reform bill of 1884) resulted in the return of eighty-six Home Rule M.P.'s in the general election of 1885.

Under Parnell's leadership the Home Rule M.P.'s were a tightly knit unit. They were pledged before the election to vote as a group on all issues. Party policy was decided by a parliamentary committee of sixteen M.P.'s, but the parliamentary committee was manipulated by Parnell and a few of his lieutenants. In the 1880's the Irish party was the best disciplined unit in the House of Commons, and its front benches probably had as much talent as either of the two British parties. The financial practices and the discipline of the Irish party were influential in shaping the development of the party system in Britain.

Obstruction was a short range parliamentary tactic. It gained Parnell the attention and loyalty of the Irish masses and discredited the assumptions that supported Butt's conciliation policy. But new rules of procedure adopted by the House of Commons to meet the problem of obstruction limited the opportunities of the Irish party to emphasize Irish grievances by delaying the passage of British legislation and Irish coercion bills. After 1880, with an increase in size and discipline, the Irish party had more interesting possibilities. Parnell decided to use the party as a balance of power in the House of Commons. In 1885 the votes of Home Rule M.P.'s forced the Liberals out of office. Parnell then supported a minority Conservative Government under Lord Salisbury, who promised not to apply coercion to Ireland. The Conservatives also agreed to initiate a program of land purchase, to investigate the possibility of more local self-government for Ireland, and to appoint a friendly Lord Lieutenant. Lord Carnarvon, who believed in a mild form of Home Rule for Ireland, became Lord Lieutenant, and the

Ashbourne act provided that the Government would lend tenants five million pounds at 4 percent interest, over a forty-nine year repayment period, to purchase their farms.[4]

While the Salisbury administration attempted to appease Irish nationalism with a policy of conciliation, Gladstone decided that Home Rule was the only satisfactory solution to the Irish Question. The Liberal leader was convinced that the Home Rule demand was just. He also realized that the Liberal party needed the support of Irish nationalists in the House of Commons because the imperialistic program of the Conservatives had such a powerful appeal for the newly enfranchised British masses.

The Liberals won the general election of 1885 in Britain, but the eighty-six Home Rule M.P.'s kept the Conservatives in office. Parnell had more confidence in Randolph Churchill, the bright young champion of Tory Democracy, than in cold Joseph Chamberlain, one of the heirs apparent to the leadership of the Liberal party. But in December 1885 Herbert Gladstone announced his father's conversion to Home Rule. Since the Conservatives could not top this, they abandoned the attempt to conciliate Irish nationalism, made Unionism the main plank in the party platform, and introduced an Irish coercion bill. Parnell threw them out of office, and Gladstone returned as Prime Minister. He commenced his third administration supported by an Irish nationalist-British Liberal alliance in the House of Commons.

This alliance, the most important event in British politics in the second half of the nineteenth century, made the Irish Question the key issue in political debate and compromised the independence of the Irish party. From 1885 on, Irish self-government was wedded to the fortunes of British Liberalism, and Parnell and his colleagues had no choice but

---

[4] Carnarvon with Salisbury's approval actually discussed possible Home Rule solutions to the Irish Question with Parnell. This did not mean the Conservatives were committed to Home Rule.

to uphold their allies in Parliament. The compact between the Irish nationalists and the British Liberals also altered the character of British party politics.

When Gladstone committed the Liberal party to Home Rule, he clarified the ideological basis of British Liberalism. In the 1860's, 1870's, and early 1880's there were still too many representatives of the Whig landed gentry tradition in the Liberal party to permit an uncompromising commitment to political, social, and economic reform. Ideological tensions within the party tarnished its image as a vehicle of progress and retarded efforts to capture the loyalty of the recently enfranchised working class. But the Whig element in the Liberal party could not digest the Home Rule alliance. They seceded from the Liberal party, called themselves Liberal Unionists, and eventually found their way into the Conservative fold. There they were at home with people who shared similar views concerning class distinctions, property rights, and the integrity of the Empire. Before the alliance between the Irish and Liberal parties, the British party system was still heavily influenced by hereditary allegiances. Home Rule, by pruning the Liberal party of its landed gentry tradition, made social, economic, and imperial issues more significant in the contest between British parties. Home Rule made it easier for the Liberal party to make a commitment to democratic advances and the welfare state. Since the vast majority of Irish nationalist M.P.'s were sympathetic to extensive social reforms and the triumph of democracy, their alliance with British Liberalism was a natural coalition that served the interest of both parties.[5]

[5] The Irish party did not necessarily embrace the total program of British Liberalism. Representing a predominantly Catholic country, the party could not accept the secular theories of education endorsed by advanced Liberals. As spokesmen for an agrarian country, Home Rule M.P.'s were more interested in the problems of the Irish masses, the tenant farmers, than in the troubles of the British masses, the industrial workers, and they were not passionate free traders like most British Liberals. Home Rulers did not share the Evangelical zeal or conscience

The Home Rule issue also served the interests of the Conservative party. It pushed the Whigs into an alliance with the Conservatives, increasing the party's strength in the House of Commons, and it provided Conservative leaders with an opportunity to exploit the no-Popery and anti-Irish ingredients of British nativism. They could attack the Liberals with such slogans as "Home Rule is Rome Rule" and argue that Irish self-government was the first step along the road leading to the destruction of the British Empire.

The British economy began to decline in the period after 1870, and factory workers and miners in Scotland and Wales were more interested in bread and butter issues than in Home Rule and Empire. Therefore, until the advent of the Labour party, the Celtic fringes of Britain remained loyal to the Liberals, but the Protestants of Ireland and the people of rural England were influenced by Home Rule to identify with the Conservative party. In order to emphasize the Home Rule issue, exploit no-Popery, demonstrate a commitment to the Empire, and attract the allegiance of the secessionists from the Liberal party, the Conservative leaders rechristened their party the Unionist party.

In many ways Parnell's Irish party was the fulfillment of the strategy recommended by Charles Gavan Duffy to the Irish Confederation in 1847 and to his colleagues in the

---

that motivated so many Liberals. They did not consider alcohol a vice and they criticized Liberal efforts to curb its consumption and at the same time raise revenue by imposing heavy taxes on the liquor industry and trade. Home Rule views on this subject were much influenced by the fact that brewing and distilling were important industries in Ireland. When it came to the support of causes associated with human freedom and dignity, the Home Rule M.P.'s were in advance of the majority of the Liberal party. The destruction of the House of Lords, as an obstacle to democracy, and a democratic suffrage had been a part of Irish nationalism since O'Connell's time. The Irish party fought for the rights of people who lived in the underdeveloped parts of the Empire and were more in sympathy with the agitation for women's rights than were the Liberals. In general, the Irish party was friendly to the welfare state direction of the New Liberalism.

independent Irish party of the 1850's. Tenant grievances had been exploited to revive Irish nationalism and to create an influential Irish party in the House of Commons. From another point of view, Parnell's Irish party was something less than Duffy's proposal. The Protestants of Ireland were not persuaded to make common cause with Catholics, and the realities of politics compromised the independence of the Irish party. To achieve reform and Home Rule Parnell found it necessary to enlist the support of a British party. From 1886 on, the success of Irish nationalism depended on the success of British Liberalism, and Home Rule was in somewhat the same relationship to Liberalism as O'Connell and his party were to Whiggery in the 1830's.

On April 8, 1886, Gladstone introduced the first Home Rule bill into the House of Commons. According to the provisions of the bill, there would be an Irish executive and parliament in Dublin with control over local affairs, but matters concerning foreign and imperial policy, the Crown, peace and war, customs and excise, the post office, coinage and legal tender, and trade and navigation were left to the jurisdiction of the Imperial Parliament at Westminister. Technically, the Irish legislature was to have only one house, but it would be divided into two orders; the smallest was designed to represent the Protestant minority, and its veto over legislation would protect their economic, political, and religious interests. Irish M.P.'s would not sit at Westminister unless it became necessary to revise the provisions of the Home Rule bill. Irish judges were to be appointed by the Irish Government and paid from the Irish Exchequer, which was also obligated to contribute to the costs of the Empire. Decisions from Irish courts were subject to appeal to the Privy Council in London, which could also decide on the constitutionality of bills passed by the Irish parliament.

This modest proposal was accepted by the Irish party, but a number of British M.P.'s argued that it was unfair to deny Ireland representation in the Imperial Parliament since 40 percent of Irish taxes would be collected by the British Government and spent for imperial purposes.[6] Conservatives attacked the bill as a concession to Irish extremism and a threat to the necessary connection between Ireland and Britain. They also insisted that the Union was essential to the maintenance of the Empire. But the fatal blow to the Home Rule bill was delivered within the Liberal party. Hartington led the Whig opposition against the bill, and Joseph Chamberlain, leader of the Radical contingent in the party, convinced that Home Rule threatened the existence of the Empire and bitter because Gladstone had given him a minor position in the Cabinet, also spoke out against Home Rule. On June 8, 1886, at the close of the debate on the second reading of the bill, ninety-three Liberals, most of them Whigs, voted against Gladstone and put him and his Irish allies in the minority 343 votes to 313.

Gladstone dissolved Parliament and took the Home Rule issue to the British electorate. The Conservatives used No-Popery, anti-Irish British opinion as a weapon against the Liberals. Lord Randolph Churchill cynically exploited Irish Protestant hatred of Irish Catholicism. He encouraged Protestants in the North of Ireland to resist Home Rule, even if it was passed by Parliament. In "playing the Orange card", Churchill coined the slogan "Ulster will fight and Ulster will be right." When the election results were in, the Conservatives had 316 seats, the Liberal Unionists seventy-eight, Home Rule Liberals 191, and Irish nationalists eighty-five. With the support of the Liberal Unionists, the Conservatives

[6] Irish party M.P.'s opposed certain provisions of the bill: customs, the imperial contribution, the temporary British control over the Royal Irish Constabulary, and voting by orders in the Irish Parliament. They expressed their criticisms in the House of Commons, but they voted for and praised the bill during the first and second readings. They did not push their objections because they knew that opposition within the Liberal party threatened Home Rule, and they had to give Gladstone their full support.

were able to form a Government, with Lord Salisbury as Prime Minister.

In 1893, in his fourth and final administration, Gladstone again introduced a Home Rule bill. This time he attempted to eliminate one of the criticisms of the first one: Ireland would have representation at Westminster during discussion of Irish and imperial questions. The second Home Rule bill passed through the House of Commons, but was defeated in the House of Lords. Gladstone wanted to dissolve Parliament and fight an election on the issue of the veto power of the House of Lords, but other Liberal leaders disagreed with this strategy. This and other conflicts with his colleagues forced the old man to resign as Prime Minister and leader of the Liberal party. Lord Rosebery, lukewarm on Home Rule and strong on Empire, replaced Gladstone as Prime Minister. During the crisis in Parliament and in the Liberal party over the second Home Rule bill and the House of Lords, the Irish party's influence was considerably weaker than it was in the 1880's. Since December 1890 Home Rule M.P.'s and Irish national opinion had been divided into Parnellite and anti-Parnellite factions.

At the beginning of 1890 Charles Stewart Parnell was at the height of his popularity in Ireland; in fact he had even won the respect of a considerable portion of British opinion.[7] In 1887 the London *Times* had published a series of articles on Parnellism and crime. They claimed that Parnell and other leaders of the Irish party were responsible for violence and agrarian crime in Ireland. In one of these articles, the *Times* reproduced a letter with Parnell's signature condoning the murder in 1882 of Lord Frederick Cavendish, Chief

[7] For political, health, and personal reasons Parnell was not a very active politician from 1886 to 1890. Most of the work of the Irish party and the nationalist movement was left to able lieutenants: John Dillon, William O'Brien, Timothy Healy, Justin McCarthy, Joseph Biggar, Thomas Sexton, and T. P. O'Connor. Dillon, O'Brien, and Healy were all young and talented. The first two were very popular for their efforts in the agrarian agitation of the late 1880's.

Secretary for Ireland, and his Under-Secretary, T. H. Burke. These men were killed while strolling in Phoenix Park, Dublin, near the Viceregal lodge, by a group of fanatical physical force nationalists who called themselves "the Invincibles."[8] The *Times* attack on the integrity of Parnell intensified antagonism to the Home Rule leader and his cause in Britain, thereby strengthening the Unionist position which the *Times* represented. Parnell was indifferent to British opinion, and he ignored the articles, but a former colleague of Parnell, now an opponent, F. Hugh O'Donnell, who was also mentioned in the *Times* articles, sued the newspaper for libel. During the trial the attorney for the *Times* made public more incriminating letters allegedly signed by Parnell.

Parnell decided to move against the newspaper, but he had no confidence in the justice of British courts and juries when they considered cases involving Irish nationalists. Therefore, he asked the Government to create a parliamentary committee of inquiry to investigate the authenticity of the letters. The Conservative Government denied his request, but did appoint a committee of three judges to investigate all of the charges made by the *Times* against Irish nationalism. During the hearing it was discovered that the *Times* had bought the letters in good faith from a Dublin journalist, Richard Pigott, a man with a shady reputation in nationalist circles. In February 1889 Pigott entered the witness box and Charles Russell, Parnell's counsel, in an example of brilliant cross-examination, demonstrated that Pigott had forged the letters. Pigott left the country and committed suicide in a Madrid hotel. The *Times,* that most respectable newspaper, was in disgrace, Irish opinion rejoiced that its leader had evaded and exposed a vile Unionist plot, and many Britons, with their notions of justice and fair play,

---

8 Parnell was most disturbed about the murders and believed that they were an attempt to discredit his work. He thought of leaving politics, but was persuaded by Gladstone to stay on as leader of Irish nationalism.

also believed that Parnell had almost been a victim of a foul conspiracy involving the *Times,* the Conservatives, and the Liberal Unionists. When Parnell entered the House of Commons following the exposure of Pigott, he received a standing ovation in which Gladstone and the Liberal M.P.'s participated.

On December 24, 1889, about ten months after Parnell's triumph over the *Times,* Captain William O'Shea, one time friend of Parnell and former Irish M.P., sued his wife Katherine for divorce on grounds of adultery, and named Parnell as corespondent. Parnell's relationship with Mrs. O'Shea was known by Liberal leaders.[9] They had used her as an intermediary in negotiating the Kilmainham Treaty. A number of Home Rule M.P.'s also knew that Katherine O'Shea was Parnell's mistress. This was made clear in 1886, when Parnell permitted O'Shea to win a Galway seat even though he refused to take the Home Rule pledge. But in the Victorian period there was a great deal of difference between a quiet affair and a public scandal. A messy divorce case could ruin a politician; one had destroyed the promising career of Sir Charles Dilke, a man many thought would succeed Gladstone as leader of the Liberal party.

Parnell told frieds in the Irish party that the divorce trial would prove that his long romance with Mrs. O'Shea was honorable. A number of people believed that the divorce case, like the *Times's* accusation, was a Unionist scheme to discredit Home Rule and its leader. A number of public bodies in Ireland passed resolutions endorsing Parnell, and the divorce case dropped from public discussion for ten months.

On November 17, 1890, the judge gave O'Shea a favorable decision in a case not contested by his wife or Parnell. O'Shea's testimony claimed that his wife and his former

[9] Mrs. O'Shea had been Parnell's mistress since 1880. In nine years they had three children, one of whom died.

friend had deceived him for over ten years, and that Parnell had restorted to all sorts of low intrigues in his deception. Historians have gathered evidence to indicate that O'Shea and his wife were on bad terms before she met Parnell, that he knew that his wife was Parnell's mistress, and for his cooperation he had received an allowance from his wife and a seat in Parliament from Parnell. He decided to sue for divorce when a legal obstacle prevented him from receiving a large sum of money his wife inherited from her aunt's estate. Parnell decided not to contest the divorce since this was the only way he could get rid of O'Shea and make Katherine his wife.[10] This decision cost him his two children by Mrs. O'Shea, who were awarded in custody to O'Shea, and it left British opinion with a sordid portrait of the Home Rule leader.

In Ireland the first reaction to the divorce decision was favorable to Parnell. The Irish National League met and endorsed his leadership, but Michael Davitt, in the *Labour World*, asked him to resign as party chairman, and Cardinal Manning of Westminster advised Gladstone to repudiate the Home Rule leader.[11] The most powerful influence work-

[10] In 1931 Henry Harrison, a Parnellite M.P., published *Parnell Vindicated*, which presented evidence revealing the true relationship between Parnell and the O'Sheas. Other historians mentioned in the Recommended Readings have evaluated Harrison's evidence and other material and have reached conclusions favorable to Parnell and critical of O'Shea. Mrs. O'Shea intended to divorce her husband and marry Parnell, but hesitated to do so when her aunt, Mrs. Benjamin Wood, was alive. Mrs. Wood was wealthy and provided the O'Sheas with a substantial income. Had she known about her niece's relationship with Parnell, she might have cut off the allowance and disinherited her. O'Shea kept quiet to protect his income. Mrs. Wood died in 1889, and Mrs. O'Shea hoped to buy a divorce from O'Shea for 20,000 pounds. Unfortunately the estate was tied up in legal problems, O'Shea did not get his money and then sued for divorce.

[11] Manning often acted as a go-between in negotiations between Gladstone and the Irish Catholic bishops. The Cardinal looked upon the Irish party as an instrument to further Catholic causes in Britain and Ireland. He was not warm toward Parnell and advised the Irish bishops that they should not permit a lay Protestant to speak for Irish nationalism. The divorce scandal appeared to him as an opportunity to destroy Parnell's control over Irish opinion and to elevate the position of the Irish bishops.

ing against Parnell was righteous and puritan British non-conformist opinion. British Liberals depended on the Non-conformist vote and Nonconformity issued an ultimatum: disassociate the Liberal party from the adulterer or lose the next general election. Political expediency dictated Glad-stone's choice.

On November 25 the Irish party was to meet and elect its chairman for the coming parliamentary session. The day before the meeting Gladstone informed John Morley and Justin McCarthy, vice-chairman of the Irish party, that Parnell would have to step down for the sake of the Irish-Liberal alliance and for the good of Home Rule. Morley failed to see Parnell before the Irish party meeting, but McCarthy delivered the Liberal leader's message. Parnell ignored the ultimatum, McCarthy didn't mention his inter-view with Gladstone at the party meeting, and the Home Rule M.P.'s, in ignorance of the issue at stake, unanimously re-elected Parnell as their leader. The next day Gladstone made public his position, and then a large number of Home Rule M.P.'s forced Parnell into calling another meeting to discuss the party leadership. From December 1 through December 6 the Irish party met in a committee room of the House of Commons and debated whether they should retain or depose the man who raised constitutional nation-alism from the ashes, achieved considerable reform legisla-tion for Ireland, made the Irish party a powerful force in the British Parliament, and forced the Liberal party to endorse Home Rule.

If Parnell had been a far-sighted, selfless, dedicated pa-triot, logic would have demanded that he gracefully abdicate as party leader to save the alliance with the Liberals and the cause of Home Rule. He would still have been a powerful force in the Irish party, and after a few years of public penance he could have returned as its leader. But Parnell was not made that way. He was a man of intense pride with a lust for power. His ruthlessness and ego had made his political fortune as they had created the power of the Home Rule movement. Parnell believed that he was the leader of the Irish nation not through election but through conquest. He had defeated Butt, the Fenians, and apathy, and he was not going to abandon his empire at the dictate of the British puritan conscience or its public spokesman, William Ewart Gladstone.

Parnell's most articulate supporter, John Redmond, argued that if the Home Rule M.P.'s deposed their leader on the urging of Gladstone, the Irish party would publicly surrender its independence and acknowledge a satellite position in relation to the Liberal party. Parnell told his colleagues that if they were going to sell him out, they had better make sure that Gladstone offered them a good Home Rule bill as the price. Parnell's opponents countered with the position that when Parnell consummated the alliance with the Liberals in 1886 the identities and the fortunes of the Liberal and Irish parties became indistinguishable and the fate of Home Rule rested on the Liberal party's appeal to the British electorate. The British electorate had spoken, Gladstone had no choice but to obey, and the Irish party had no option but to depose Parnell and elect a new leader. On December 6, Justin McCarthy left the committee room followed by fourty-four Home Rule M.P.'s, leaving Parnell with twenty-seven.[12] The anti-Parnellite majority moved into another room and elected McCarthy as their party chairman.

Parnell refused to retire. He decided to appeal over the head of the Irish party to the Irish people. This brought in the influence of the Irish Catholic bishops and priests as the deciding factor in the conflict dividing Irish nationalism.

---

[12] Some of the prominent members of the Irish party were in the United States collecting funds during the party crisis. O'Brien and Dillon could not return home because they would be arrested under the crimes act for their work in the agrarian agitation, the Plan of Campaign. They and most of the American delegation supported the demand that Parnell resign.

On December 4, during the debate over Parnell's leadership the bishops issued a manifesto to the Irish people asking them to reject him. The bishops' manifesto did not influence the Irish party, which made a political, not a moral decision. In the contest for the loyalty of the Irish masses, the Catholic clergy emphasized the moral question and not the future of the Liberal alliance. Since the Protestants of Britain had denounced Parnell as a public sinner, an enemy of the sanctity of marriage, Catholic bishops and priests, who had always placed a high premium on sexual morality, could hardly appear to be less pious.

In 1891 Parnell put his prestige on the line in three Irish by-election contests. He never worked harder or more courageously as he vigorously campaigned for Parnellite candidates, but he was overmatched by the combination of the Catholic hierarchy and clergy, the anti-Parnellite majority of the Irish party, and Gladstone. Parnell's candidates lost all three elections, and Parnell ruined his health campaigning in the cold and damp of Ireland. He died in Brighton of rheumatic fever on October 6, 1891, and was buried close to O'Connell in Glasnevin cemetery, Dublin. The dead chief left behind him a shattered Irish party, a disillusioned and divided Irish national opinion, and the powerful myth of a martyred messiah—a myth that would inspire future generations of young people, particularly writers and poets. Parnell as myth was even more powerful than the Parnell of reality.

From the defeat of the first Home Rule bill in the summer of 1886 until December 1905, the Liberal party was in power less than three years (August 1892–February 1895). Lord Salisbury was the Unionist Prime Minister from 1886 to 1892 and then again from 1895 to 1902. When he left office he was succeeded by his nephew, Arthur J. Balfour, who as Chief Secretary for Ireland, 1887–1891, designed the Irish policy followed by the Unionist Governments.

Balfour and Salisbury agreed that the primitive Irish

masses were not ready for the responsibility of self-government and that Home Rule for Ireland would threaten
Britain's European defenses, lead to the eventual collapse
of the Empire, and create a Catholic dominated anti-Protes-
tant Irish Parliament. The Conservative leaders controlling
the coalition that made up the Unionist party exploited the
religious issue to arouse Irish and British hostility to the
Irish nationalist-British Liberal alliance. They also rallied
property interests behind the Unionist standard by identifying Home Rule and Irish nationalism with radical democracy and socialism.

But the Irish policy of the Unionist Government was not
solely based on repression of Irish nationalism and preservation of the status quo. Balfour, a tough Chief Secretary,
believed that Ireland had to be cowed into subservience by
a long period of resolute government. His efficient use of the
crimes act to suppress agrarian outrage and agitation won
him the name of "Bloody Balfour" in Ireland. That name,
however, represents an unfair estimate of Balfour's contribution to Ireland. In the twenty-year period dominated by the
Unionist party, Balfour tried to achieve the same results in
Ireland with methods similar to those tried by Peel in the
1840's. He believed that Irish nationalism was a synthetic
movement that would collapse once the economic needs of
the peasant masses were realized. Demands by Liberal
Unionists for Irish reform created pressures within the
Unionist party in support of Balfour's program of coercion
mixed with conciliation.

In his effort to "kill Home Rule with kindness" Balfour
did satisfy many of the demands of tenant farmers. Despite
the land act of 1881 and Ashbourne's land purchase scheme
of 1885, the agricultural depression which started in the
1870's continued on into the 1880's, with the usual pattern
of eviction, agrarian agitation, and violence. In 1887 Balfour
introduced a land act which lowered rents to match prices

and offered increased protection against eviction. The next year he produced another land purchase bill, the first in a series of measures leading to the final Unionist land scheme of 1903. George Wyndham was the Chief Secretary who brought in the final bill, which encouraged landlords to sell with a 12 percent cash bonus and tenants to buy with low interest rates and a sixty-eight-and-one-half year repayment period. Six years later the Liberal Government amended Wyndham's bill to include compulsory sales in certain circumstances. Land purchase proved to be the final solution to the land question. The legislation of 1903 and 1909 created 200,000 peasant proprietors whose farms amounted to about half the arable land of Ireland.

Balfour was as interested in eliminating poverty and raising the standard of living as he was in solving the land question. In 1891 he established the Congested Districts Board to provide relief and to stimulate the growth of the Irish economy in the most depressed sections of the country. Most of the Board's activities were concentrated in Connacht, but good work was also done in Kerry and Cork. Using Government subsidies, the Board encouraged the development of cottage industries (spinning and weaving), fishing, and agriculture. Many of the achievements of the Board were accomplished through extensive programs of technical and agricultural education. The Board consolidated many small farms into efficient agricultural units, placed poor farmers on these units, and taught them to work the land efficiently. Experts agree that the work of the Congested Districts Board made a substantial contribution to economic progress and a rise in the Irish standard of living. It was probably the most intelligent, successful, and humane product of British rule in Ireland during the nineteenth century.

In addition to the poverty program of the Congested Districts Board, Balfour initiated a number of public works projects to provide employment and to stimulate the Irish economy. These projects successfully concentrated on railroad construction, road and bridge building, and drainage. A Unionist Government, constantly warning against the socialism of the Liberal party, was carrying on a welfare state project in Ireland far in advance of anything yet attempted in Britain.

Although the Unionists did not relent in their hostility to Home Rule as the final solution to the Irish Question, they did make a major concession to the Irish demand for local control over domestic affairs. The local government act of 1898 stripped the Protestant gentry dominated grand juries of all fiscal and administrative powers and responsibilities and transferred them to the jurisdiction of popularly elected urban, rural, and county councils. These local government bodies gave Irishmen as much control over local affairs and appointments to local office as enjoyed by the people in Britain. The local government act was intended by the Unionist Government as a substitute for an Irish Parliament. Instead, the experience of managing local business provided a training ground for Home Rule and encouraged the expectations of Irish nationalism.

When the Unionists left office in December 1905, only the university education question remained of all the economic, social, and religious issues used by Irish nationalists to stimulate anti-British attitudes and to perpetuate the demand for Home Rule.[13] Nevertheless, the progressive legislation passed by the Unionist Government did not destroy the demand for self-government. The Balfour-Salisbury view of Irish nationalism as only a reflection of economic and social discontent

[13] The university education question was finally settled by the Liberals. In 1908, the Royal University of Ireland (a new name for Queens, 1879) was dissolved and replaced by the National University of Ireland. The old Queen's colleges in Cork and Galway became colleges within the National University and, in 1909, University College, Dublin, opened its doors. Queen's College, Belfast, remained as an independent university.

was obviously superficial and unrealistic. In contrast, Gladstone understood that Irish nationalism had assumed an identity independent of those grievances which created and nourished it. He knew that the Irish Question could only be resolved by conceding some measure of Home Rule. The Conservative refusal to consider an Irish Parliament, and their exploitation of religious and property prejudices to strengthen Unionism, made a final settlement of the Irish Question more difficult for both Britain and Ireland.

CHAPTER SIX

The Crisis of Irish Nationalism, 1906-1914

In 1900 the split in the Home Rule movement that began with the Parnell divorce scandal in 1890 came to an end. After long negotiations John Dillon, leader of the anti-Parnell nationalist M.P.'s, graciously stepped aside and John Redmond, commander of the small Parnellite minority, was elected chairman of the re-united Irish parliamentary party. Reunion increased the influence of Home Rule M.P.'s in the British House of Commons, made it easier for the party to appeal to the Irish at home and abroad for funds, and strengthened nationalist morale. But the Irish party after 1890 never enjoyed the same degree of devotion that the Irish people gave to it when Parnell was "The Chief".

The divorce scandal, followed by the party split, disillusioned some nationalists and made others cynical about politics. After party unity was restored, these people were psychologically incapable of transferring to Redmond the emotional commitment they had once given to Parnell. And, of course, by 1900 the Irish party was over twenty-five years old. The bloom of youth had left the Home Rule cause. Those energetic and militant young men who followed Parnell to Westminster in the early 1880's to fight for Irish freedom in the camp of the enemy were now middle-aged, respectable politicians. Their devotion to Home Rule remained intact, but their enthusiasm had been tempered by the give and take of parliamentary experience and compromise. Home Rule M.P.'s had done good work for their constituents. They had forced the Liberal party to endorse Irish self-government and Parliament to pass legislation improving every aspect of life in Ireland. These successes were appreciated in Ireland, and if the parliamentary party was not the exciting force that it was in 1890, it still enjoyed the overwhelming support of Irish nationalist opinion. The Home Rule M.P.'s, however, had become so involved with the routine of parliamentary activity that they began to lose intimate contact with the people they represented. When they started to think like British politicians, they became insensitive to the undercurrents of Irish life.

John Redmond was an excellent chairman for a party in the House of Commons; he was intelligent, respected by the leaders and backbenchers of the British parties, and a skillful and effective debater. He also possessed superior degrees of integrity and courage, both of which were tested in the 1890's when he remained loyal to Parnell at great personal sacrifice and risk. But Redmond had a serious flaw for a leader of Irish nationalism. Like the founder of the Home Rule movement, Isaac Butt, he had too much respect for Parliament, the British Constitution, British codes of conduct, and British institutions. Redmond also shared Butt's admiration of the Empire as an agent of civilization. He took pride in Ireland's many contributions to the creation and maintenance of the Empire. He was sincere when he argued that Home Rule would strengthen rather than weaken Ireland's ties with Britain and the Empire. When not in the House of Commons, whether in London or at his home in Wicklow, Redmond was a shy man, an introvert who enjoyed privacy and the companionship of only a few close friends.

He relished the parliamentary aspect of political life, but disliked public meetings and the demagoguery essential to the leader of a popular cause, one that depended on the enthusiasm and financial generosity of the Irish masses.

The emphasis on political nationalism by the Irish party, and the style of its leadership, did not satisfy the emotional or psychological needs of all Irish nationalists. In the 1890's there was a revival of the spirit of Young Ireland. Cultural nationalists insisted that political independence was not the most pressing need of their country. They asked: what would be accomplished if Ireland had her own Parliament in College Green, but Irishmen remained British in culture and values? To be truly free, Ireland must be de-Anglicized. She must revive her own language, culture, and traditions; she must recover her own soul. Cultural nationalism inspired three significant movements: the Gaelic League, the Gaelic Athletic Association, and the literary revival.

Since the time of Young Ireland in the 1840's, there had been efforts to preserve the Irish language where it existed and to revive it where it had perished. In 1893 the Gaelic League was founded, with Douglas Hyde of County Sligo, a graduate of Trinity College, as the dominant personality in the movement. Hyde, the son of a Protestant rector, was raised in an Irish-speaking district. He learned the language and cultivated the literature and traditions of the people. He devoted his life to the language movement and in 1889 published the first in a number of volumes of translations of Gaelic stories and poems. With the establishment of the National University in 1908, Hyde was appointed to the Chair of Modern Irish at University College, Dublin. Hyde originated the slogan "the de-Anglicization of Ireland". He insisted that Irish must be preserved as the national language of the country. The Gaelic League was devoted to this and to the study and publication of Gaelic literature. It also encouraged the development of a contemporary literature in the Irish language.

The League flourished, and by 1903 there were over 500 branches in the country. Members of the League learned Irish, read Irish literature, played Irish music, sang Irish songs, and danced Irish dances. On their annual holidays they traveled to Irish-speaking districts in Waterford, Donegal, Kerry, Connacht, and the Aran Islands to polish their language skills in conversations with native speakers and to absorb Irish culture and traditions at their peasant roots. Gaelic Leaguers often became intolerant toward Irishmen who were indifferent to the language revival, calling them "West Britons."

Hyde attempted to keep the Gaelic League independent of politics. Self-government was of secondary importance to cultural independence. Hyde wanted the Gaelic League to unite all Irishmen—Protestants, Catholics, Unionists, Home Rulers, and Republicans—in the common cause of Irish cultural nationalism. He feared that if the League became identified with any particular sect or political position its influence would be limited. Some of the Home Rule politicians considered the League a rival for the affections, and thus the financial contributions, of the Irish people, but they were forced by practical considerations to officially endorse its work and objectives.

The Gaelic League appealed to the middle class in the cities and large towns. Cultural nationalism came to the small towns, villages, and rural parishes in the form of the Gaelic Athletic Association. In 1884 Michael Cusack, the model for the Citizen in Joyce's *Ulysses*, founded the Association at Thurles, Tipperary. Archbishop J. W. Croke, in giving an episcopal blessing to the Association, condemned English sports like lawn tennis, polo, croquet, and cricket as alien and not "racy of the soil." He told Irish lads to participate in the games of their ancestors: hurling, football, running, leaping, hammer throwing, and wrestling.

The G.A.A. spread through the South and West of Ireland with parishes organizing hurley or football teams and sometimes both. Like the Gaelic Leaguers, the G.A.A. members developed an intolerance towards all things English. In order to maintain control over the youth of the country and to isolate them from foreign influences the Association denied to those participating in English games the right to share in the activities of the G.A.A. And like the League, the Association promoted the interest of cultural nationalism, thus encouraging an enthusiastic love of Ireland in contrast to the efficient but prosaic style of constitutional nationalism as represented by the Irish party at Westminster.

The revival of cultural nationalism expressed in the Gaelic League and the Gaelic Athletic Association, while important for Ireland, did not attract much outside interest. To the rest of Western Civilization, Ireland was a country with an unfortunate history and legitimate grievances against British rule, but she was too insignificant to merit serious concern or attention. Her economic development was retarded, her culture was primitive, and her people failed to make significant contributions to art or literature. Her chief city, Dublin, once a flourishing eighteenth-century capital, was now a seedy, dull, provincial town.

Then suddenly in the late nineteenth century, dreary little Dublin became one of the literary and theatrical centers of the world. The Irish literary movement took inspiration from the language revival and scholarly investigations into pre-Christian and early Christian Irish history and culture. Most of the prominent figures in the literary renaissance were Anglo-Irish Protestants (William Butler Yeats, John Millington Synge, George Russell, and Lady Gregory). Contradicting the class, religious, and political prejudices of their background, they embraced cultural nationalism.

They condemned British rule in Ireland because it discouraged a distinct, creative, and significant Irish culture. Like the Gaelic Leaguers and the Gaelic Athletic Association leaders, the Anglo-Irish writers attempted to restore the values of the ancient culture by recalling its virtues to the youth of their time.

Parnell's fall also influenced the imagination and the patriotism of Yeats and his friends. Parnell was the classic tragic hero brought down at the height of his power. He was the Irish messiah "crucified" by the people he came to liberate.[1] In using and expanding the Parnell legend, the writers attempted to prepare the way for another messiah—perhaps one of their own group—who would save Ireland and, through the Celtic genius, the rest of Western Civilization from Anglo-Saxon materialism. In glorifying the simple, unsophisticated peasant and attacking British industrialism, the writers were following the dogmas of cultural nationalism formulated by Young Ireland in the 1840's. They believed that rural Ireland contained the necessary spiritual energy to revive Irish civilization. The tillers of the soil had not sold their "racial" souls to alien materialistic influences. They preserved the folk tradition, the belief in supernatural forces—pagan as well as Christian—and the language.

[1] Some outstanding examples of Parnell's inspiration are Yeats's *Parnell's Funeral*, Lady Gregory's *Deliverer*, and James Joyce's "Ivy Day in the Committee Room" (in *Dubliners*) and his passionate Christmas dinner scene in *Portrait of the Artist*. Parnell's influence lasted beyond the literary revival as evidenced in the moving first chapter of Sean O'Casey's *Pictures in the Hallway* ("A coffin comes to Ireland"), and Sean O'Faolain's best novel, *Bird Alone*. The Parnell legend did more than inspire specific work; it created a hero, a cause, and an attitude. For the young writer fighting "tyranny"—the British, the Catholic Church, the conventions of a provincial puritan society—Parnell was the symbol of freedom and genius and also the martyr destroyed by these "tyrannies." Parnell's influence over Irish writing is discussed at length in Herbert Howarth's *The Irish Writers: Literature and Nationalism, 1880-1940* (New York, 1959), and in Donat O'Donnell's (Conor Cruise O'Brien) "The Parnellism of Sean O'Faolain," *Maria Cross: Imaginative Patterns in a Group of Catholic Writers* (New York, 1952).

Not all Irish writers were romantic or sentimental. Synge, a protege of Yeats and a supporter of Home Rule, refused to subordinate his talents or his view of truth to the myths of cultural nationalism. His earthy peasants, in contrast to the ethereal creatures of Yeats's early years, introduced realism and surrealism into the Irish theatre. James Joyce, a product of urban middle class Catholic Ireland, withdrew from the literary and language movements, and, by embracing exile, also rejected the creed of cultural nationalism. He believed that Ireland could only achieve salvation by a candid examination of the national conscience.

With the exception of George Russell (A.E.), the leaders of the literary movement were not involved with specific economic, social, or political problems, but they played a significant role in the national awakening and deserved some credit for the final victory of Irish nationalism. Their contribution, however, has often been exaggerated. Yeats and his friends did not create or solely inspire a revolution. Easter Monday 1916, and the subsequent Anglo-Irish war, were to a great degree inspired by cultural nationalism, but it was more the cultural nationalism of Thomas Davis and Young Ireland than the Celtic Twilight.[2] And there were other factors that explain Ireland's twentieth-century struggle for independence—the Republican traditions of 1848 and the Fenians, social injustice, tactical mistakes by the Irish party, and the inadequacy of British politicians.

But the literary revival did put its stamp on Irish cultural nationalism, and its writers, unlike the Young Ireland propagandists, were great artists. The quality of their creative work was unsurpassed in any country in the world. For the

---

[2] The revolutionary movement of 1916-1922 was also inspired by the Irish revolutionary tradition—1798, Robert Emmet, 1848, and the Fenians—and by economic and social discontent. Trade Unionism in Ireland with its Socialist and Syndicalist influences increased passions for freedom and reform and might have encouraged a commitment by some to physical force methods.

first time in centuries Ireland made a contribution to Western Civilization. Through the works of the writers of the revival, sophisticated and influential people in Britain, on the Continent, throughout the Empire, and in the United States learned of Ireland—her culture, her traditions, her grievances, and her demand for freedom. When Ireland fought for freedom world opinion was with her, and world opinion finally convinced British politicians that they must extend a measure of independence to nationalist Ireland.

With the literary movement, the Abbey theatre, and the Gaelic League, Dublin, during the two decades preceeding World War I, experienced an intellectual excitement and energy she never knew before and might never know again. Sinn Fein, the brain child of journalist Arthur Griffith, also contributed to the intellectual vitality of the period.

In 1898 Griffith began to develop his Sinn Fein ("we-our-selves") policy in *The United Irishman*. He synthesized a variety of sources in developing his program for Irish self-determination: his study and interpretation of Hungarian history, the writings of Jonathan Swift, Thomas Davis, and John Mitchel, and some of O'Connell's ideas and experiments in the Repeal agitation of 1843. Griffith was a cultural nationalist enthusiastic in his support of the efforts of the Gaelic League and the Gaelic Athletic Association to de-Anglicize Ireland. He was a Republican by personal conviction, but he did not believe that Irish public opinion shared that conviction, and he was certain that Ireland could not succeed in establishing a Republic through military efforts. Griffith advised nationalists to agree on a compromise goal, a dual monarchy based on the example of Austria and Hungary.

Griffith asked Home Rule M.P.'s to admit that their attempt to win Home Rule in the British House of Commons had failed. He advised them to follow the example of Francis Deak, the Hungarian nationalist, who in 1867 refused to recognize the sovereignty of the Austrian legislature. They should leave Westminster and establish a parliament in Dublin, as was suggested by O'Connell in 1843. The Irish government would have the loyalty of local governmental boards and agencies, and it could set up its own courts of law modeled on O'Connell's successful experiment with arbitration courts. Confronted with a de facto Irish government and a determined passive resistance to continued British rule and occupation, Britain would have to retreat from Ireland and recognize her independence. Ireland would then be associated with Britain only through a common allegiance to the monarch. After independence was established, the Irish Parliament would encourage the growth of the Irish economy with legislation protecting native industries, since sovereignty must be economic as well as cultural and political.[3]

In Griffith's writing it was possible to detect the provincialism and intolerance inherent in cultural nationalism. He praised the work and the goals of the Gaelic League and the Gaelic Athletic Association, but he was suspicious of the writers associated with the literary movement. Griffith and many other cultural nationalists inherited the Young Ireland position that writers and intellectuals must subordinate their genius to the aims of Irish nationalism. Literature should help create a sound nationalist opinion, publicize Irish grievances, and justify self-government. When writers presented Irishmen or Irish life as less than ideal, they insulted their country and weakened the national effort. Griffith and many of his friends, including some creative writers, joined the attack on Synge's *Playboy of the Western World*. Not too many years later, cultural nationalists would abuse

---

[3] Griffith's protectionist leanings were probably influenced by reading the works of the German economist Friedrich List, but there was a protectionist tradition in Irish nationalism. O'Connell was a free trader and the Irish party was tied to the Liberal free trade tradition, but the Young Irelanders supported the Corn Laws as essential to Irish agriculture.

Sean O'Casey for his interpretation of life in the Dublin tenements.

Before World War I Sinn Fein was not a serious rival to the parliamentary party's hold on Irish nationalist opinion. But its program attracted the interest of many intelligent and dynamic young people disenchanted with the style of the parliamentary party and filled with a desire to do something for Ireland. And Sinn Fein caught the attention of the Irish Republican Brotherhood, which was seeking methods to undermine the influence of Home Rule on Irish opinion.

Although the I.R.B. had a small membership in the United Kingdom at the beginning of the twentieth century, there were active centers in Dublin and British cities, and they had contacts with the Clan-na-Gael in the United States. The strategy of the Republicans in the period before World War I was to recruit dependable and intelligent young men and to whittle away at constitutional nationalism. They appreciated the possibilities of the revival of cultural nationalism. They infiltrated the Gaelic League and the Gaelic Athletic Association and moved into responsible positions. Republicans joined Sinn Fein when it became an organized movement in 1905 and persuaded Griffith to drop Dual Monarchy as the official political objective.[4] Instead, Sinn Fein adopted an open policy in regard to the future constitution of Ireland. Few in numbers but strong in conviction, Irish Republicans were on the move, and by 1914 they were in a good position to determine the direction of Irish nationalism—if the Irish parliamentary party made any serious mistakes.

Another factor in a slowly changing Irish climate of opinion was the militancy of labor. Dublin in the early twentieth century had more social problems than any large city in the

---

[4] The revised 1917 Sinn Fein constitution endorsed a Republic as the goal of Irish nationalism.

United Kingdom, and Dublin's problems were typical of those in all Irish cities. One-third of her population lived in slum tenements, most of them unfit for human habitation. A surplus labor supply meant large scale unemployment. Employers exploited the situation by paying salaries far below the standards established in Britain. Sub-human living conditions, inadequate diets, unemployment, and low wages all encouraged alcoholism, prostitution, and other vices and produced a high death rate, with tuberculosis and infant diseases as the major killers.

James Larkin, a Liverpool-born Catholic Irishman with an Ulster family background, and a Socialist with Syndicalist leanings, made a valiant effort to give dignity and financial security to the lives of the Irish urban proletariat. In 1908 he organized the Irish Transport Workers Union, and by 1912 he had recruited about ten thousand men representing a wide variety of skills and occupation. Through skillful negotiations, an iron will, and the use of strikes, Larkin won a series of major victories over the Dublin employers, and these victories increased salaries and bettered working conditions for members of his union.

In August 1913 Larkin's union began a strike of the Dublin United Tramway Company. William Martin Murphy, chairman of the Tramway Company—the wealthiest man in Ireland, with extensive economic interests in Britain and the Empire—decided to destroy Larkin's influence. He organized the employers of Dublin against the Transport Workers Union. By September 1913 the Employers Federation Limited had locked 25,000 workers out of their jobs. The strike lasted until January 1914, when finally the employers' combination, the hostility of the Catholic hierarchy, and the reluctance of British trade unions to continue financial support forced the workers back to their jobs, often on the stringent anti-union terms of the bosses.

Larkin was defeated in 1914, but the Dublin strike provided insights into the character of the Irish Question and helped create a revolutionary spirit in nationalist Ireland. The decision of the British Trades Union Congress to limit its support of the strike indicated that the British proletariat was unwilling to make sacrifices for Irish workers in the cause of class solidarity. National prejudices were stronger than class loyalties. This gulf that divided the working class in Britain from the proletariat in Ireland reflected the lack of understanding that people from all classes in Britain had for Ireland and the Irish people. The defeat of 1914, and the indifference of British labor opinion to economic and social injustice in Ireland, forced the Irish worker to become more nationalistic and revolutionary. Many believed that only a revolution completely destroying British influence in Ireland would clear the way for a transformation of Irish society.

Liberal party leaders in the years following the defeat of the second Home Rule bill were reconsidering their involvement with Irish nationalism. Since Gladstone's time, the party had been too committed to the principle of Home Rule to denounce Irish self-government, but many influential leaders decided that it would be wise to deemphasize Irish self-government as a major or immediate objective of Liberal policy. They believed that the Chamberlain Radicals and the Whig imperialists who deserted the Liberal party on the issue of Home Rule could be persuaded to return by a Liberal program emphasizing social reform and commitment to Empire.

At the turn of the century the Irish nationalist-British Liberal alliance was strained by Irish support for the Boers and the decision of the Irish parliamentary party to adopt a more independent stance in the House of Commons. The pro-Boer opinion of Irish nationalism offended British public opinion and the imperialist wing of the Liberal party, thus encouraging Liberal leaders to retreat from the Home Rule issue.

In the general election of 1906 the Liberal party won an

overwhelming victory at the polls. With their large majority in the House of Commons Liberal leaders did not need the support of the Irish party, so they decided to avoid the unpleasant fate of previous Liberal administrations which had tried to satisfy the demands of Irish nationalism. They did not repudiate the Liberal commitment to Home Rule, they just ignored it.[5] Turning away from the Irish Question, Liberals decided to appease a demand for radical social reform which had been building up in Britain since the decline in Britain's economic strength during the 1870's. The restless spirit of British opinion was reflected in the Liberal victory and in the election of twenty-nine members of the recently formed Labour party to the House of Commons. In response to the challenge of Socialism, the Liberal Government passed through Parliament a program to alleviate many of the social security burdens of the working class. This welfare legislation necessitated large expenditures of money at a time when taxpayers were also being asked to reconstruct the British navy to meet the threat of German jingoism and militarism.

In his search for new sources of revenue, Lloyd George, Chancellor of the Exchequer and the bright young man of the Cabinet, resorted to schemes originally suggested by the Fabians. He recommended substantial duties on the unearned income of landed property, higher income taxes for the wealthy, and, to please the Non-conformist element in his party as well as to raise revenue, increased taxes on liquor and tobacco.

Unionists in the House of Commons lacked sufficient

[5] In 1907 the Liberals did offer Irish nationalists an Irish council bill. The bill proposed to establish a council in Ireland composed of elected and appointed members with the Lord Lieutenant as an ex-officio member. The council would have a generous Government grant and the power to coordinate and control the efforts and goals of Government agencies in Ireland. On the instruction of an Irish convention, the Irish party rejected this offer of self-government as an inadequate payment of the Liberal pledge to Home Rule.

strength to halt the advance of the welfare state or to resist this attack on wealth and property, so they used their majority in the House of Lords to frustrate the program of New Liberalism. In violation of established tradition, the Lords culminated their series of vetoes by rejecting Lloyd George's budget, thus precipitating a grave constitutional crisis. Liberal leaders decided to use this rash and unprecedented defiance of the election returns and constitutional precedent to destroy the absolute veto of the Lords. The budget with its heavy duties on liquor injured the important brewing and distilling companies in Ireland, but Irish nationalist M.P.'s viewed the Lords as the major obstruction in the path of Home Rule and were more than eager to help the Liberals emasculate the upper house. Labour M.P.'s objected to the hereditary House of Lords as a citadel of property rights and a barrier to the classless and planned society. They joined the Irish in supporting the Liberals in the great battle for democracy.

In January 1910 Herbert Asquith, the Prime Minister, took the issues of the budget and the veto to the country. The returns from the general election (275 Liberals, 273 Unionists, eighty-two Irish nationalists and forty Labour M.P.'s) shattered the compacency of the Ministry. Why did the same electorate which had given the Liberal party a 224 seat advantage over the Unionists in 1906 reduce that lead to two only four years later, particularly after the Liberals had provided an extensive program to relieve the poverty of the proletariat and had announced their intention of eliminating the most glaring undemocratic feature of the Constitution? Did many middle class and rural Liberal voters object to the collectivist character of the Government's welfare program and the means of financing it through taxes on property, did members of the working class resent paying more pennies for their pints and smokes, did the increased Labour vote and representation in Parliament mean that trade union leaders considered the Government's welfare program inadequate, was the House of Lords more popular with the public than the Government supposed, were Britons apprehensive concerning German naval and military power and the international crises that seemed to push Europe closer to war? There is evidence to indicate that all of these factors influenced voters, but it is also true that the Irish Question played a significant role in the revival of the Unionist party. Although Liberals played down the Home Rule issue in their election addresses, their opponents emphasized that a successful assault on the veto of the House of Lords would be followed by a Liberal attempt to dissolve the Union with Ireland.

In November 1910, after the Lords attempted to avoid catastrophe by passing the budget, Asquith, after consulting with the new King, George V, decided to ask the electorate for a second opinion on the veto power of the House of Lords. This time 272 Unionists were returned to match an equal number of Liberals, and the Asquith Ministry found itself deeper in bondage to its Irish and Labour allies who controlled eighty-four and forty-two seats respectively. More accurately the Irish party had the allegiance of seventy-five M.P.'s; nine Irish M.P.'s referred to themselves as independents and followed the leadership of either William O'Brien or Tim Healy. In this election Home Rule received equal attention with the House of Lords. Asquith, speaking in Dublin, pledged Liberal support for Home Rule, and during the campaign Unionists described the Prime Minister as the pawn of John Redmond. They warned British voters that the fate of the Union was tied to the future of the House of Lords.

The general elections of 1910 gave the Irish parliamentary party the balance of power in the House of Commons. And the combined Liberal and Labour representation in the House of Commons indicated that British opinion, by a slight majority, was prepared to accept Home Rule for Ireland. But the revival of the Unionist party in these elections was evidence that a considerable portion of the British population retained its fanatic opposition to Irish independence.

After considerable prodding from the Irish and Labour benches, the Government, in February 1911, introduced a bill limiting the power of the House of Lords to a three-session or two-year suspensive veto over legislation passed by the House of Commons. When the peers realized that the King, if need be, would honor his pledge to Asquith and pack the Lords with Liberals to secure passage of the Parliament bill, they agreed to submit to the inevitable. The path was now clear for Home Rule, and Irish nationalists had delivered a fatal blow to their old enemy, the House of Lords. In addition, they had helped remove an important obstacle to the evolution of political democracy in Britain.

Asquith introduced the third Home Rule bill in the early spring of 1912. He recommended a mild federal proposal which would place local affairs in the hands of a Dublin parliament consisting of a popularly elected lower house, with a set number of representatives from each of the four Irish provinces, and a senate nominated in the first instance by the Crown and subsequently by the Irish Executive. Ireland was to retain a small delegation at Westminster to protect her Imperial interests. The Irish Parliament was to be restricted in legislating on questions involving finance, foreign affairs, religion, and police powers. Protestant rights were to be guaranteed in a number of ways: Ulster would be overrepresented in the lower house of the Irish Parliament, the appointed senate would no doubt contain a large Protestant representation, and the Irish Parliament could not endow or show favoritism to any sect.

Redmond and Irish nationalist opinion accepted this limited Liberal offer of self-government as a settlement of Irish claims. Even Sinn Fein moderated its criticism of the

Irish party, and, for a time, a truce existed between the various factions within Irish nationalism. Protestant Ireland, however, was opposed to Home Rule, and Irish Protestants would be the decisive factor in the Home Rule crisis.

During the eighteenth century Irish patriotism was associated with the Protestant aristocracy and middle class. Their volunteer movement forced the British Government in the 1780's to make substantial concessions to Irish demands for independence. Protestants were the leaders of the United Irishmen of the 1790's, who embraced the radical Republicanism of revolutionary France. Many Protestants in Northeast Ulster participated in the rebellion of 1798.

By 1800 Protestants in Northeast Ulster began to realize the economic possibilities involved in a Union with Britain. The spirit of the United Irishmen began to fade as an interest in Union grew. Protestants in other Ulster counties, areas where the Catholic-Protestant populations were more evenly balanced or where Catholics had a majority (Donegal, Cavan, Monaghan, Armagh, Fermanagh, and Tyrone), were hostile to the Union. Like many Protestants in Leinster, Munster, and Connacht, they believed that Protestant Ascendancy could best be protected in a Dublin Parliament. From 1798 to 1800 Orange lodges were active in the campaign against the Union, while Catholic opinion tended to look to the proposed Parliament of the United Kingdom for an objective hearing of their claims.

As the nineteenth century progressed, Irish Protestant opinion became increasingly committed to the Union. Northeast Ulster was absorbed into the British industrial complex; linen making and ship building flourished, and Belfast became the most prosperous city in Ireland. With the rise of O'Connell's nationalist movement, a popular agitation built on Catholic grievances, Protestants in all sections of Ireland feared that an independent Ireland would be dominated by a radical Catholic democracy. Their militant attachment to the Union was based on a conviction, perhaps more emotional than rational, that only the British connection could protect their religious, political, and property rights.

Irish Protestants were absorbed into the no-Popery stream of British Toryism. They were used as a garrison protecting British interests in Ireland. In the early nineteenth century Tory Governments rewarded the loyalty of Irish Protestants by defending their monopoly of political, economic, and social power and retaining the privileged position of their Established Church. After the emergence of Irish nationalism, Irish Protestants fought all Government concessions to Irish agitation. They were used as pawns in British Conservative efforts to frustrate Irish reform policies proposed by the Whigs, Peel, and Gladstone. Lord Randolph Churchill encouraged British Unionists to "play the Orange card" in opposing Gladstone's Home Rule bills.

No-Popery and Unionism produced an Irish Protestant nationalism and made it impossible for Protestant landlords, middle class people, and members of the working class to cooperate with Catholics of the same classes to further programs of mutual interest and to promote the progress of their common country. No-Popery and Unionism practically destroyed Liberalism in the Irish Protestant community, particularly in Ulster, and retarded movements for social, economic, and political reform. Reform was subordinated to Protestant solidarity, and this left the landed aristocracy and the big businessmen in control of Irish Protestant opinion. Of course there were exceptions. People like Sharman Crawford, Isaac Butt, and Charles Stewart Parnell demonstrated that all Protestants were not motivated by narrow class and religious interests.

Despite the efforts of Irish Protestants to resist the pressures of Irish Catholic and nationalist opinion, Whig, Liberal, and even Unionist attempts to pacify Ireland gradually undermined Protestant Ascendancy, transferred ownership of land to Catholic peasants and control of local government in Leinster, Munster, Connacht, and part of Ulster to the Catholic majority. Each Government concession to Irish nationalism strengthened the Irish Protestant belief that only the Union could protect their rights as a minority in Catholic Ireland.

After John Redmond announced Irish nationalist support for the third Home Rule bill, Irish Unionist leaders Sir Edward Carson and Sir James Craig made it clear that since the Parliament act would make it impossible to resist the demands of Irish nationalism with constitutional weapons, they were prepared to employ revolutionary tactics to frustrate Home Rule. They rejected the Home Rule bill as detrimental to the interests of Irish Protestants. They said that they would not consent to any legislation that severed the religious, economic, cultural, and patriotic ties that bound them to Protestant Britain or forced their allegiance to a Dublin parliament dominated by Anglophobe Papists determined to discriminate against a helpless Protestant minority.

Carson and Craig quickly demonstrated that they were not bluffing. In September 1912 they led Ulster Protestants in signing a Solemn League and Covenant binding Irish Unionists to resist Home Rule with every means at their disposal. Soon an Ulster Volunteer Army began drilling under the command of Lieutenant-General George Richardson, K.C.B., and on September 23, 1913, Ulster Unionists announced plans for a provisional government. Carson was to be chairman, and the new administration was to go into effect the day Parliament passed the Home Rule bill for the third time. Instead of repudiating words and deeds which threatened armed resistance to an act of Parliament, Andrew Bonar Law, leader of the Opposition, and other British Conservatives gave an unqualified endorsement to Carson's attack on constitutional government. They promised British

Protestant support for any Irish Protestant effort to defeat Home Rule and Irish nationalism. Bonar Law and many other British Unionists, while sympathetic to the Ulster Protestant position on Home Rule, exploited the Irish issue to force a general election. Balfour, the former Prime Minister, represented a Conservative faction that was not emotionally attached to the Ulster Protestants, but "played the Orange card" to preserve the Union.

As the Home Rule bill made its stormy way through Parliament in the sessions of 1912, 1913, and 1914, events in Britain and Ireland confirmed fears that the Government could not enforce the Home Rule bill in Northeast Ulster without risking the probability of civil war. Every day the Ulster Volunteers gained in strength and efficiency, and a successful gunrunning operation in April 1914 supplied them with valuable equipment to wage war. Added to the Government's difficulties was the distinct possibility that army officers would refuse to move against the Ulster Volunteers if so ordered. Under the existing military system, army officers usually came from the same class that provided the Unionist party leadership, and it was only natural that they should entertain all the opinions and prejudices of their class. Under the British system of government, however, the army is nonpolitical and is expected to carry out the orders of the civilian Government without questioning their validity. In designating suppression of rebellion in Ulster as an exception to their duties, British officers permitted themselves a luxury denied enlisted men. Labour M.P.'s and Irish and British labor leaders complained that if enlisted men from the working class were used by the Government as strike breakers, officers should not be exempted from enforcing laws offensive to the aristocracy.

In the period 1912–1914 many men in the upper echelons of the military establishment conspired to defeat the parliamentary process. Lord Roberts, Chief of Staff, recommended

Richardson to Carson as Commander-in-Chief of the Ulster Volunteers and later congratulated the Irish Unionist leader on the success of the gunrunning operation. Sir Henry Wilson, an Ulster Protestant and Director of Military Operations, advised Carson and Craig to persist in their opposition to Home Rule. He consulted with Bonar Law on ways in which the Opposition could amend the army appropriation bill to prevent the use of military force against the Ulster Volunteers. Prominent Conservative politicians and army leaders were encouraging rebellion in the army at a time when it appeared that a major war might break out on the Continent, a war that would probably involve Britain, since she was so heavily committed to France. The unreliable state of the army was made clear to all in March 1914, when officers stationed at the Curragh, County Kildare, announced their intention to resign their commissions as an alternative to leading troops against the Ulster Volunteers. Since Asquith was reluctant to weaken Britain's military strength in a period of international tensions, the officers escaped punishment.

Probably the most formidable obstruction to Home Rule was the militant pro-Unionist, anti-Irish, anti-Catholic sentiment that pervaded Britain. Pro-Home Rule British opinion was lukewarm; anti-Home Rule opinion was fanatic. Public meetings, newspaper and periodical editorials, sermons from Protestant pulpits, petitions to Parliament, and a pattern of Unionist by-election victories indicated that many Englishmen were willing to support Ulster's resistance to Home Rule, even to the extent of civil war.

Confronted by armed rebellion in northeast Ulster, "treason" in the army, pro-Unionist-no-Popery opinion in Britain, and waning Liberal strength in the House of Commons, some Cabinet members like Winston Churchill and Lloyd George lost their zest for the struggle and recommended that concessions be made to Ulster. As early as 1913 they suggested that portions of Ulster containing Protestant majorities should be excluded from the Home Rule settlement. And by 1914, Asquith openly admitted that partition of Ulster was the only feasible alternative to civil war. Two questions remained undecided: was exclusion to be temporary or permanent, and how much of Ulster would remain outside the jurisdiction of the Irish Parliament?

Asquith obtained Redmond's consent to a six-year exclusion for any Northeastern Ulster county (presumably Armagh, Antrim, Derry, and Tyrone) indicating by plebiscite a desire to maintain the British connection. This solution to the Ulster question was in theory a temporary partition of Ireland and a compromise between the positions of Irish nationalists and Unionists. In fact, it became permanent partition and a major concession, if not a surrender, by Redmond. By the time the six years were up in 1920 there would be at least two general elections, and political trends indicated a Unionist victory at the polls in 1915. A Unionist majority in the House of Commons could then permanently exclude the four Ulster counties from the jurisdiction of the Home Rule bill. But Sir Edward Carson was a stubborn man. He demanded permanent exclusion from the beginning for all nine counties in the province of Ulster. This was an outrageous claim since the province had returned a nationalist majority to the House of Commons, and Catholics outnumbered Protestants in five of the nine counties. At the King's request, negotiations on the principle of exclusion of at least part of Ulster took place at Buckingham Palace in the summer of 1914. Since Carson and Redmond could not agree on time limits and boundaries, the conversations concluded without a settlement. Asquith could go no further in his effort to appease Ulster without encouraging a rebellion in nationalist Ireland.

In late 1913, nationalist Ireland began to lose patience. As nationalists observed the growing armed might and defiance of Ulster Protestants, the pro-Unionist activity of military leaders, hostile anti-Irish demonstrations in Britain, a series of Liberal defeats in British by-elections, and the Government's willingness to compromise the principle of a united Ireland, they became increasingly apprehensive and restless. The Irish party had played and won the parliamentary game, but it appeared that Ireland would be denied the trophy of victory.

Nationalists in the South decided to imitate the tactics of Carson to demonstrate to the Liberals that they were as determined as the Orange militants in Ulster. During the Dublin strike the Transport Workers Union organized a citizen army to protect strikers from police brutality, and in the fall of 1913 the Irish Volunteer Army was formed in Dublin by a committee representing various shades of nationalist opinion—Home Rule, Sinn Fein, and Republican. The Irish Republican Brotherhood encouraged the formation of the Volunteers, and the I.R.B. members quickly occupied key positions in the Volunteer administration.

The Irish Volunteers, modeled on the patriot force of the 1780's, were not organized as a revolutionary army prepared to initiate a war for Irish independence. They were established to defend the constitutional right of Ireland to have Home Rule against the unconstitutional intimidation of Ulster and British Unionists. Volunteer leaders wanted to make it clear to wavering British Liberals that Irish nationalists were as determined to fight for freedom as Irish Unionists were to frustrate the establishment of an Irish Parliament. While most Volunteers hoped that their action would keep peace by strengthening Liberal resolve, no doubt there were physical force nationalists in the Volunteers looking for an opportunity to prove their patriotism in battle.

At first Redmond viewed the Volunteers as a nuisance and a threat to the Irish party, but when he finally realized that Asquith might compromise Home Rule to appease Carson and anti-Irish British opinion, he publicly endorsed the military movement and obtained a deciding voice in its operation. In July 1914 he won for the Irish party the right to nominate half the members of the Volunteers executive committee. Redmond forced the Volunteer leaders to make this concession by threatening to establish a rival organization. The patronage of the Irish party stimulated Volunteer enlistments and encouraged the financial support of Irish-Americans. In January 1914 the Irish Volunteers had only 10,000 or so recruits, but after Redmond took charge enlistments increased to over 15,000 a week. The United Irish League of America promised the Irish party leader that the Volunteers would have all the money they needed to defend the Home Rule cause.

Asquith now appeared to be caught in an inescapable dilemma. Home Rule had to be carried in some form or the Liberals would forfeit the Irish alliance and control of the Government. But a Home Rule bill that did not guarantee permanent exclusion to Carson and his British Conservative allies would provoke an insurrection in Ulster. One that did would encourage rebellion in nationalist Ireland. In either case, civil war would engulf Britain and Ireland. Asquith did have two other alternatives. He could call another general election, but all the signs indicated that the results would still keep him a prisoner of the Irish and Labour parties, or he could resign and surrender office to the Unionists. Since Bonar Law could not command a majority in the House of Commons, he would not be able to govern without the cooperation of Asquith and other moderate Liberals. A national coalition might have been able to steer Britain through the Home Rule crisis, but it would have alienated not only Irish but also Labour and left wing Liberal support from the Liberal party. By the summer of 1914 parliamentary government had obviously broken down in Britain, and the politicians found themselves at the mercy of forces not responsible to the House of Commons.

Since Carson would not budge from his impossible demand for all of Ulster, Asquith decided to proceed with the original plan for a six-year exclusion of the four Northeast counties of Ulster from the jurisdiction of the Irish Parliament. He told the British electorate that six years would demonstrate the success or failure of Home Rule for the rest of Ireland, and, in the meantime, they would have at least one and probably two opportunities to express their wishes on Home Rule for all of Ireland. The Prime Minister's exclusion proposal was introduced as an amending bill in the House of Lords, but the Unionist majority among the peers modified the exclusion amendment to include all of Ulster on a permanent basis and returned it to the House of Commons.

Asquith scheduled July 27 for a debate on the amending bill, now without a time limit, a further concession to Bonar Law and Carson, agreed to by Redmond, but violence in the streets of Dublin forced a postponement. On Sunday, July 26, a company of Irish Volunteers unloaded a cargo of arms from a yacht near Howth. The arms were purchased in Hamburg by the anti-Redmond faction in the Volunteers without the knowledge of the Irish party leader. When the Volunteers were on their way back to Dublin, their path was blocked by the assistant commissioner of police and a battalion of the King's Own Scottish Borderers demanding that the nationalists surrender their rifles. The front ranks of the Volunteers held off the British soldiers with their rifle butts, permitting their comrades to drift away with the weapons. When the frustrated Borderers returned to Dublin, they were in a touchy mood. As they marched down Bachelor's Walk, a sidewalk crowd shouted insults at them, and a few people threw stones at the soldiers. Suddenly a small number of Borderers lost control of themselves and started to fire into the crowd. Three people lost their lives, and thirty-six others were wounded.

The next day Redmond in the House of Commons asked

the Government to delay debate on the amending bill so that an investigation could be made of the violent incident in Bachelor's Walk. In the course of his speech, he asked why the Ulster Volunteers were permitted to display publicly their smuggled guns in the north of Ireland, while similar action by the Irish Volunteers in the south resulted in an exhibition of military force. It was an excellent question, and the Government could not provide a satisfactory answer. Instead, as usually happens in these cases, the politicians found a scapegoat. The assistant commissioner of police, David Harrel, admitted that sending troops to disarm the Volunteers was illegal, so he and the commanding officer of the Borderers were censured by a judicial committee of inquiry.

The delay in the amending bill debate and Austria's declaration of war on Serbia, followed by the mobilizations of the Continental powers and Germany's declarations of war on Russia and France, turned the attention of the House of Commons and the British public away from Ireland toward the Continent. When the Foreign Secretary, Sir Edward Grey, informed Parliament on August 3 that Germany's threat to Belgium neutrality and Britain's commitments to France made probable a war against the Central Powers, John Redmond, with patriotic enthusiasm, told the House of Commons that nationalists in the south of Ireland would be glad to join with Orangemen in a common defense of their country against a possible foreign invasion. The leader of Irish nationalism, the successor of O'Connell and Parnell, was cheered on all sides as a defender of British interests, which he sincerely believed in 1914 were the interests of freedom and civilization.

After Britain entered the war Asquith and his Cabinet colleagues decided to shelve the Irish Question for the duration. To win Irish nationalist cooperation for the war effort, Home Rule was placed on the statute books, but with

Redmond's consent the Prime Minister attempted to appease Unionists with a suspensory bill delaying the operation of Home Rule until after the war was over.

Britain had narrowly escaped civil war, but British politicians had not solved the Irish Question; they had only postponed a decision. Neither the leaders of the British political parties nor the Home Rule M.P.'s realized that the stalemate of August 1914 would so alter the character of Irish nationalism that a final answer to the Irish Question could never be worked out through parliamentary procedures or within the framework of the Empire.

CHAPTER SEVEN

The Rose Tree, 1914-1922

*There's nothing but our own red blood
Can make a right Rose Tree.*[1]

John Redmond, chairman of the Irish parliamentary party,
considered World War I a conflict between good and evil.
Germany represented authoritarianism, militarism, and contempt for the integrity of small nations. Redmond believed
that Ireland should assist Britain and France in the effort
to preserve representative government and demonstrate her
concern for the unfortunate plight of Belgium. By making
a sacrifice for the principle of freedom, Ireland would show
Britain and the world that she had the capacity for self-
government. Redmond urged members of the Irish National
Volunteers to enlist in the British army. To Sinn Feiners and
Republicans in the Volunteer movement, the contest between
Britain and Germany was a naked struggle for power and
not a crusade against tyranny. Ireland had no grievance
against Germany; she was occupied and oppressed by
Britain. Why should young Irishmen risk their lives to
promote the interests of the British Empire? They should
remain at home and prepare to exploit Britain's international
problems by pressing their own country's claims for freedom.
When the war started there were about 180,000 Irish

Volunteers; only 12,000 of them refused to endorse the war views of Redmond. The majority who remained loyal to the Home Rule leader were called the National Volunteers, and many of them enlisted in the British army. Eoin Mac-Neill, professor of early Irish history at University College, Dublin, was commander of the minority group, which retained the name Irish Volunteers. Unknown to MacNeill, the Irish Republican Brotherhood controlled key positions in the Irish Volunteers and decided its strategy. Padraic Pearse, I.R.B. director of organization, poet, barrister by training, and Master of St. Enda's school, where instruction in the Irish language was emphasized, was the link between the military council of the I.R.B. and the Irish Volunteers.

Shortly after the war began the I.R.B. hierarchy decided to organize a revolution against the British Government to take place before the conclusion of hostilities on the Continent. This revolution would demonstrate Ireland's commitment to independence and earn her consideration in any general European peace settlement. John Devoy, leader of the Clan-na-Gael in the United States, participated in the planning for the revolution and contacted the German ambassador in Washington, who promised the aid of his government. Sir Roger Casement, an Ulsterman who had completed a brilliant career in the British civil service, went to Germany from the United States to obtain material support for a rising and to recruit Irish prisoners of war for a brigade to fight for Irish freedom. The Germans promised aid, but did not take Casement too seriously, and only a very small number of Irish prisoners of war were interested in the Irish brigade. Other I.R.B. envoys, however, made an impression in Berlin and were able to get solid guarantees of guns and ammunition.

Pearse and other poets in the I.R.B.—Joseph Mary Plunkett

1 William Butler Yeats, "The Rose Tree," *Collected Poems* (New York, 1944), 210-11.

and Thomas MacDonagh—were romantic revolutionaries and did not consider victory the significant objective of the coming rebellion. In their poetry they insisted that Ireland needed a blood sacrifice to raise her from the apathy which had resulted from the failures of the Irish parliamentary party and constitutional nationalism. If a group of young men would demonstrate their eagerness to shed their blood and die for Irish independence, the fire of nationalism, dampened into embers by Home Rule, would blaze again. The first group to offer their lives for Ireland would inspire others to take up their mission and eventually drive the British out of Ireland. A blood sacrifice would create a revolutionary Irish opinion, which would permeate the country and wipe out the disgrace of centuries of foreign occupation.

After James Larkin left for the United States in October 1914 to raise money for the Irish Transport Workers Union, James Connolly, an Irish Catholic socialist sympathetic to syndicalist tactics, took command of the union and its Citizen Army. There were only about 200 men in the Citizen Army, but Connolly perfected their discipline for the coming revolution. Connolly was planning revolution independent of the I.R.B., and he had no use for romantic notions about blood sacrifice. He believed that the Citizen Army and the Volunteers could catch Britain by surprise while she was concentrating on the Continental war and, with a quick military success, rally the Irish people behind the revolution. Faced with a united, disciplined, and armed revolutionary Ireland, Britain would evacuate the country, clearing the path for an Irish Socialist Republic.

In the early years of the war Redmond retained the loyalty of most of the Irish people, but his influence slowly and steadily declined. Lord Kitchener, who was in charge of the war office, did most to destroy the position of the Irish party and its leader. Kitchener had no use for Irish nationalism and refused to woo its support for the war effort. He permitted the Ulster Volunteers to enlist as an Ulster division with their own officers and emblem, the Red Hand of Ulster. But he would not let the National Volunteers join up as a separate unit with their own Catholic officers and insignia, the gold harp on a green field. Before the fighting was over in France two Irish divisions from the South were in action, but they were commanded, for the most part, by British and Irish Protestants. Kitchener's policy was considered in Ireland as a calculated insult, and it seriously limited recruiting efforts in Leinster, Munster, and Connacht. World War I was not popular in Ireland, and heavy Irish casualties in the Gallipoli campaign increased apathy toward recruiting efforts. The reorganization of the British Government in 1915 was also unpopular in nationalist Ireland. In order to increase national unity, Asquith invited Unionists and Irish nationalists into the Government. Redmond, loyal to his nationalist principles, refused to participate in a British administration, but Carson, Bonar Law, and F. E. Smith (later Lord Birkenhead)—old and fanatic enemies of Home Rule—did join the Government. Irish nationalists did not welcome the authority of a Government under Orange influence.

The Irish Volunteers and the Citizen Army drilled in the mountains and held public reviews in the streets of the cities. Sinn Feiners and Republicans organized anti-recruiting campaigns; their newspapers emphasized the need for Irish neutrality in the conflict between the Allies and the Central Powers and advised Irishmen not to become involved in Britain's war. British authorities, anxious to avoid violent incidents like Bachelor's Walk, permitted the drilling and parading, but jailed or deported some Sinn Feiners and Republicans and closed down extreme nationalist newspapers. Most of the suppressed newspapers soon reappeared under new names.

Republicans finally set a day for the revolution, Easter Sunday (April 23), 1916. Connolly joined the Military Coun-

cil of the I.R.B., and the Germans promised to land guns
and ammunition during Holy Week on the South coast of
Ireland. Pearse persuaded MacNeill to call for a general
review of all Volunteer units with full military equipment
on Easter Sunday. Plunkett helped forge a British Government document indicating that the authorities were preparing to raid the headquarters of the Irish Volunteers, the
Citizen Army, Sinn Fein, and the Gaelic League and to
arrest their leaders. This document, which may have represented British intentions, was used by the I.R.B. to ready
MacNeill and the Volunteers for a defensive war without
revealing the plans for a rebellion.

MacNeill finally learned of the I.R.B. plans for Easter
Sunday, but when Pearse informed him that German equipment was on the way, he decided to go along with the
revolution and turn control of the Volunteers over to the
I.R.B. But Casement was captured by the Royal Irish
Constabulary in Galway shortly after coming ashore from a
German submarine, and when the German ship, the *Aud*,
arrived off the coast of Kerry on Good Friday, no Volunteers
appeared to unload her cargo. While she waited, the *Aud*
was intercepted by British warships. Her captain scuttled
her, and the obsolete Russian rifles and the ammunition for
them went to the bottom of the sea. When the news of
these disasters reached Dublin on Holy Saturday, MacNeill
decided the revolution would fail and canceled the orders
to mobilize and march on Easter Sunday. Pearse, determined
on a blood sacrifice, insisted on proceeding with the rising,
although he knew that he would have few troops at his
disposal. He hoped that an insurrection in Dublin would
inspire the rest of the country to take up arms. Connolly
also made up his mind to lead the Citizen Army into action.
He thought the revolution still might succeed because he
naively believed that British capitalists would not destroy
private property to subdue Irish rebels.

On Easter Monday a force of 1,528 rebels, twenty-seven of

them women auxiliaries, marched through the streets of
Dublin and then seized the General Post Office and other
strategic buildings. From the balcony of the Post Office
Pearse read a document proclaiming the Irish Republic.
This proclamation was then posted throughout the city and
a Republican tricolor flag of green, orange, and white was
hoisted on the flag pole of the Post Office.

From Monday until they surrendered on Saturday the
rebels held off the police and the army, which was quickly
reenforced from Britain. The fighting was vicious and
intense, and British casualties were heavy: 103 soldiers,
fourteen members of the Royal Irish Constabulary, and three
men from the force of the Dublin Metropolitan Police were
killed; 357 soldiers, twenty-three constabulary men, and
three policemen were wounded; and nine soldiers were
missing. Only fifty-two members of the Volunteers and the
Citizen Army were killed, but 450 Dublin civilians were
killed and 2,614 wounded by stray bullets and shells. Connolly was wrong: "Britannia's sons with their long range
guns" bombarded the city and many buildings were destroyed by fire and shells.

The rebellion did not inspire the Irish people to join the
fight for freedom. While the rebels fought a hopeless war
against the British army, many Dubliners took advantage
of the chaos to loot shops, and at Westminster Redmond
condemned the rising as a German plot involving only a
fanatical and misguided minority of the Irish population.
"Respectable" Irish opinion considered the Republicans and
Sinn Feiners as dirty traitors. This sentiment was conditioned
by the fact that a considerable number of Irish people had
husbands, brothers, sons, friends, and sweethearts fighting
with the British army in France. When Republican prisoners
were marched along the street on their way to gaol, people
lining the way cursed and jeered them.

Then came the reprisals. Over a period of ten days the

leaders of the rebellion were court-martialed and executed. Connolly was so badly wounded that he was shot strapped to a stretcher. Thirteen others, including Pearse, Plunkett, Clarke, MacDermott, and MacDonagh, were also shot.[2] More than 2,000 Sinn Feiners and Republicans were imprisoned in Ireland and Britain, many of them without trials. Execution of "traitors" in time of war is a common thing, but the long period of time taken for the court-martials and executions made it appear that Britain had adopted a policy of sadistic revenge and terror. And the imprisonment of so many men, without normal legal procedures, seemed cruel and arbitrary. Within a few weeks the "dirty traitors" of Easter week had become gallant martyrs and national heroes. Their pictures were displayed in Irish homes; their speeches and poems were widely sold, read, and quoted. As Yeats said in a poem written shortly after the rising, "A terrible beauty was born." Pearse was right: a blood sacrifice had raised Ireland from apathy. Nationalism was intensified, and the Irish people began to turn their backs on the Irish party and constitutional methods. The Republic, the bullet, and the grenade would soon replace Home Rule, the ballot box, and parliamentary debates as the goal and methods of Irish nationalism.

Easter week forced the British Government to reassess the status of the Irish Question. In 1916 Britain was attempting to persuade the United States to enter the war against the Central Powers, but anti-British Irish-American opinion was influential in the Democratic party. Lloyd George, who would soon replace Asquith as Prime Minister, was assigned the task of pacifying Ireland. He decided on the immediate application of the Home Rule bill with the exclusion of six Ulster counties until the Ulster Question could be settled

---

[2] Casement was tried and executed in Britain, and another man was shot for revolutionary activities in Cork during Easter week, so the total number of martyrs was sixteen.

by the postwar Parliament. This plan was frustrated by Unionist opposition, and Redmond withdrew his blessing when he became convinced that Lloyd George intended the permanent partition of Ireland.

When immediate Home Rule proved politically inexpedient, the Government attempted to cool the Irish situation by releasing the Sinn Fein and Republican prisoners. By the end of the war all had returned home. Eamon DeValera, a mathematics teacher, had commanded a Volunteer unit at Boland's Flour Mill during Easter week and was sentenced to execution. Because he was born in the United States, the influence of Washington was able to commute his sentence to life imprisonment. DeValera's prestige as the only surviving Easter week commandant brought him recognition as the leader of Republican nationalism. When he returned home, he received the admiration of the Irish masses. De Valera set out, with other released prisoners, to reorganize the Volunteer army and to contest Irish by-elections under a Sinn Fein party label. Before the end of the war, Sinn Fein had won seven elections, but the victorious candidates refused to take their seats in the House of Commons.

When the United States entered the war in the spring of 1917, American leaders warned the British Government that it would be difficult to enlist maximum American energy behind the Allies as long as the Irish Question remained unsolved. To satisfy American opinion, and to get Irish support for the war, Lloyd George, now Prime Minister, summoned an Irish Convention representing all shades of opinion—Sinn Fein, Home Rule, and Unionist—to work out an acceptable proposal for Home Rule. Southern Unionists were prepared to cooperate in creating an Irish Parliament, but Ulster Unionists, encouraged by their colleagues in Britain, blocked all roads to harmony. Redmond was so generous in his willingness to make concessions to Irish Protestant opinion that he antagonized some important Catholic nationalists. The Convention held its first session in July 1917 and concluded in stalemate in April 1918. A month before the Convention ended in failure, John Redmond died of complications following a routine gall stone operation. The Home Rule leader was too exhausted and disillusioned to wage a successful struggle for his life.

By late 1917 the brutal conflict on the Western Front had taken a heavy toll of British manpower. With Russia ready to make peace, Germany could concentrate on winning a victory in the West. Britain was desperate for soldiers, and there was mounting pressure to force Ireland to contribute her young men to the war effort. In April 1918 Parliament authorized Lloyd George to impose conscription on Ireland. Immediately the Irish party walked out of the House of Commons and joined Sinn Fein, the Catholic bishops, and the trade union in a common front against conscription. The anti-conscription campaign strengthened the Republican movement, speeded up the reconstruction of the Volunteer army, and forced Britain into a tougher policy of coercion. Many Sinn Feiners were deported or, like DeValera, sent to prison, but the war ended without Britain applying the draft to Ireland.

The post-Armistice general election, held in December 1918, brought a coalition Government victory in Britain and a Sinn Fein triumph in Ireland. Sinn Fein won seventy-three seats to six for the Irish party and twenty-six for the Unionists.[3] Sinn Fein M.P.'s refused to take their seats in the British House of Commons. They met in Dublin and organized an Irish Parliament, Dail Eireann, which began to administer the country in the name of the Irish Republic. The Dail established arbitration courts to supersede the British legal system, a board to settle industrial disputes, and

[3] Despite the election victory there is reason to doubt that Sinn Fein had the unanimous support of nationalist Ireland. Many constituencies were not contested, and in those that were only 69 per cent of the eligible voters cast ballots and just 47 per cent of them voted Sinn Fein.

a land bank to make loans to people wishing to purchase farms; and it sent delegates to the Versailles Peace Conference to plead the case for an independent Irish Republic. But the great defender of national self-determination. Woodrow Wilson, refused to antagonize his British allies, and the Irish delegates were ignored.

In February 1919 Michael Collins, who had done most to revive the Volunteer army, and Harry Boland, another member of the Sinn Fein executive board, helped DeValera escape from Lincoln gaol in England. DeValera returned to Ireland in March, was elected president of the Dail in April, and in June left for the United States to raise money for the Republic. He remained in the United States until December 1920. In his absence, Arthur Griffith served as acting president of the Dail. Collins was in charge of finances, but he retained his rank and duties as adjutant general and director of organization for the Volunteers; Cathal Brugha was minister of defense and Volunteer chief of staff. There was friction between Brugha and Collins; perhaps the former was jealous of the latter. Collins' brilliant intelligence network, his daring escapes, and his dashing personality made him the popular hero and overshadowed the important work of the chief of staff.

The shooting war began in January 1919, forcing Britain to supplement the Irish police force and increase the size of the army serving in Ireland. In March 1920 the British Government began recruiting ex-servicemen in England and sent them to Ireland as part of the Royal Irish Constabulary. When they arrived, a uniform shortage made them wear dark green caps with khaki shirts and pants. From their clothing they acquired the name Black and Tans. Later in 1920 Britain recruited former army officers to serve as a special auxiliary force of the R.I.C.

In the Anglo-Irish war the Irish Republican Army (the new name of the Volunteers) adopted guerrilla tactics. Young men in civilian clothing ambushed lorries, assassinated "spies" and "informers," shot soldiers, policemen, Tans, and Auxiliaries, then quickly merged into the civilian population, which sheltered rebels and refused to give information against them. British forces met terror with terror in a policy of reprisals. They burned, looted, and occasionally murdered. Republican prisoners were tried by court-martial, and a number of them resorted to hunger strikes to focus international attention on the Irish struggle for freedom. British authorities described the unconventional methods of the I.R.A. as murder, but guerrilla tactics are the only practical way for a small nation limited in resources and population to fight a war of liberation against a world power.

Britain's effort to destroy Irish nationalism was restricted by the situation. Since the British Government refused to recognize the existence of the Irish Republic, it was technically involved in a police action to put down rebellion. British leaders could not afford to admit that they were fighting the Irish nation and thus wage a total war for victory. They were attempting to fight a limited campaign against Sinn Fein without jeopardizing a future peaceful settlement with the Irish people.

World and British opinion also restricted the tactics of the Government. The reprisals by the Black and Tans and the Auxiliaries damaged Britain's image and shocked a growing section of the British community. Prominent clergymen in the Anglican Church, notably the Archbishop of Canterbury, the Asquith Liberals, and the Labour party condemned British policy in Ireland and demanded a negotiated settlement. They argued that the terror tactics of the I.R.A. did not justify the barbaric methods of reprisal. There was constant pressure from the pulpit, the Opposition benches in the House of Commons, and the left-wing press for an Irish settlement that would concede self-government to Ireland.

Reacting to this hostile opinion, Lloyd George in 1920 attempted to end the Anglo-Irish war with a better government of Ireland bill. The bill established two Irish parliaments—one for the six Northeast counties of Ulster and one for the rest of the country—and a Council of Ireland composed of representatives from both legislatures. By administering services delegated to it by both parliaments, the Council of Ireland was intended as a bridge leading to the eventual reunification of the country. The better government of Ireland bill also called for representatives of nationalist and Unionist Ireland to sit with the Imperial Parliament at Westminster.

After elections were held for the two parliaments a government was established for Northern Ireland, but in the South Sinn Fein used the election to demonstrate its control over nationalist opinion. The war continued with its ambushes, assassinations, burning, looting, and murder. Antiwar British opinion increased in strength and influence. Failing to solve the Irish Question with Home Rule and partition, Lloyd George was forced to negotiate directly with DeValera. A truce was concluded in July 1921, as a preliminary to treaty negotiations.

Early conversations in London between Lloyd George and DeValera were fruitless. The wily, pragmatic Welshman could not communicate with the more doctrinaire Irish revolutionary. When Lloyd George tried to discuss specific terms, DeValera replied with lectures on Irish history. But the Prime Minister did make it clear that he was ready to concede Dominion status with the following reservations: Britain would continue to maintain naval and air bases in Ireland and recruit Irishmen for her army and navy; Ireland would have to limit her army in conformity with the British military establishment, maintain free trade relations with Britain, and contribute to the British war debt. DeValera rejected the offer as too restrictive on Irish sovereignty, Lloyd

George then threatened war, and the Irish leader finally agreed to take the British offer back to Dublin for discussion in the Dail.

The Dail rejected Dominion status as inadequate, but DeValera said that he was not a doctrinaire Republican. Lloyd George believed that the door was still open for negotiations and scheduled a treaty conference in London before the end of the year. In a decision still debated among Irish nationalists, DeValera announced that he would not go to London, and the Dail selected Collins, Griffith, George Gavan Duffy, Robert Barton, and Eamon Duggan as its envoys. Erskine Childers, an uncompromising Republican, went along as one of the secretaries to the Irish delegation. The powers of the envoys were vague. They were commissioned to negotiate and conclude a treaty with the British Government, but they were ordered not to sign it unless its contents were first approved by the Dail. And when the Irish envoys left Dublin they had no clear definition of what would be an acceptable settlement.

When the Irish envoys began October discussions with the British delegation they confronted men experienced in all of the nuances of politics and negotiations—Lloyd George, Austen Chamberlain, Lord Birkenhead, and Winston Churchill. Lloyd George was willing to negotiate, but he was the leader of a Coalition Government dominated by Unionists who for thirty years had fought Home Rule. The realities of British politics limited the concessions that the Prime Minister could make; the Irish delegation was caught between these realities and the fanaticism of the Republicans in Ireland.

Lloyd George resubmitted his offer of Dominion status, but two issues emerged as major obstacles to a final settlement: the oath of allegiance to the British monarch and the status of Northern Ireland. The British representatives insisted that the oath of allegiance had to be part of the

Irish Free State Constitution. In reply the Irish said that they could not accept the oath but were prepared to acknowledge the Crown as head of the association of states which comprised the British Commonwealth. The principle of external association, which would have recognized an Irish Republic as a member of the Commonwealth, was DeValera's idea and has been practiced within the Commonwealth since World War II. In 1921, however, external association was not acceptable to the British. Instead, they offered to let the Irish design an oath of allegiance that would not be any more demanding than those used by other Dominions and would put primary allegiance to the Free State rather than to the Crown.

No Irish nationalist could agree to a permanent partition of his country. Lloyd George, however, made clear the difficulties involved in forcing Northern Ireland to accept the jurisdiction of the Dublin Parliament. Sir James Craig, leader of the Northern Ireland Government, would not accept such a solution, and the British Unionist majority at Westminster would endorse Ulster resistance. As a compromise, the Prime Minister suggested a Boundary Commission to survey the loyalties of the Ulster population before deciding the Free State-Northern Ireland border. Irish envoys reasoned that if Catholic nationalists in the Six Counties were permitted to choose allegiances, the Free State would acquire at least Fermanagh and Tyrone and perhaps sections of Derry and Armagh. Lloyd George told the Irish delegates that a four county Northern Ireland was an economic impossibility and that the work of the commission would inevitably lead to a united Ireland. The compromise seemed plausible and was accepted by the Irish nationalists.

During a pause in the London negotiations, the Irish delegation returned to Dublin. DeValera, under pressure from extreme Republicans Brugha and Austin Stack, refused to accept Dominion status with the oath of allegiance, and insisted that external association was the only acceptable compromise. But in early December, Lloyd George impatiently decided to intimidate the inexperienced Irish diplomats into signing a treaty. He issued an ultimatum: Dominion status or all out war. Griffith, whose original Sinn Fein program was constructed around the principle of Dual Monarchy, had no objection in principle to Dominion status. Michael Collins was convinced that the I.R.A. and the war weary Irish population were not prepared for a resumption of the conflict with the British. He considered Dominion status a major concession and a foundation for a future extension of freedom. The ultimatum might be a bluff, but Ireland was in no position to call it. With heavy hearts and many doubts, the Irish delegates on December 6, 1921, signed an agreement with the British Government establishing the Irish Free State as a Dominion within the Commonwealth.

DeValera rejected the treaty and led the opposition when it was debated in the Dail in early January 1922. When the members of the Dail completed their arguments, the treaty was ratified by sixty-four votes to fifty-seven. After his defeat DeValera resigned as president of the Dail, and Griffith was elected in his place. Within a few weeks, British officials turned over the reins of government to Free State authorities and began to evacuate a country that they had dominated for almost 800 years. Meanwhile, many I.R.A. commanders commenced a civil war against the Free State, a war endorsed by DeValera and the Republican politicians. This civil war lasted until May 1923 and was fought with more brutality than the Anglo-Irish conflict. It left scars on the Irish community which still exist. Before the Free State had succeeded in defeating the rebels and could concentrate on reconstruction and the normal routine of running a state, seventeen million pounds had been spent for military equipment, Griffith had died of a heart attack, Childers was executed as a rebel in arms, Brugha had died in battle, and Collins was ambushed and killed in County Cork.

There is room to question the tactics used by Irish Republicans in their war against Britain and even the accomplishments of that war. True, Ireland in 1922 achieved a measure of freedom in excess of the demands of O'Connell, Young Ireland, Butt, Parnell, or Redmond. But she had lost Ulster; the Boundary Commission turned out to be a farce and partition to be .permanent.[4] Perhaps Sinn Fein could have achieved Dominion status by passive resistance to British rule in Ireland, without resorting to the violent methods that created fanaticism and civil war. And a number of people still argue with some logic that Home Rule would have been granted after World War I and that it would have eventually evolved into Dominion status.

These are all debatable possibilities. We do know that there was an Anglo-Irish war that resulted in the Free State and that this war had major significance for world history. Ireland was the first country in the twentieth century to win emancipation from foreign domination through her own efforts. Ireland's struggle for freedom was a prototype for revolutionary movements all over the globe. In 1922 she faced the same problems of stability, civil war, and reconstruction that would later challenge other underdeveloped emerging nations. Like the other new nations that would come into existence in Asia and Africa, Ireland confronted the challenge of independence with young leaders trained in the ideological rigidity of revolution rather than the

4 When the Boundary Commission started work, it was made clear to the Irish Free State representative that the British Government would never alter the boundary separating Northern Ireland from the Free State to the extent that the existence of Northern Ireland would be threatened. This meant no significant change in the status quo. The Boundary Commission collapsed under the pressure of irreconcilable points of view. The Six Counties remained intact and the British Government compensated the Free State by relieving her of the obligation to contribute to the British War debt. The Irish have never considered this adequate compensation for partition.

compromise of politics. The only men in Ireland with years of legislative experience and political skill, the members of the Irish parliamentary party, were among the casualties of the Anglo-Irish conflict. Repudiated by the people, they were unable to contribute their considerable talents and common sense to a new nation that they had served so well in times of difficulty.

Conclusion

An analysis of the Irish Question, 1800–1922, has a special relevance in a world of disappearing empires, emerging nations, and cultural conflicts between affluent and underdeveloped countries. Britain's experience in Ireland was in many ways a preview of future troubles in Middle Eastern, Asian, and African portions of the Empire and would be shared, to some extent, by the French in Southeast Asia and North Africa. The current difficulties of the United States in Southeast Asia and Latin America are often reminiscent of Britain's Irish problems.

Leaders of Protestant industrial Britain and the British public were unable to bridge the cultural gap that separated them from the Catholic masses of agrarian Ireland. They could not understand that their economic dogmas and value system were not necessarily applicable to people with different problems and historical traditions. As a result, Britain was slow to respond to the needs and demands of Irish opinion. This failure to find an early solution for the religious, economic, social, and political problems, fused in that maze called the Irish Question, left a vacuum to be occupied by Irish nationalism.

Irish nationalism, built on Catholic grievances and extended to include a wide range of issues, in time forced

Britain to realize the emergency character of the Irish Question. Britain's efforts to destroy Irish nationalism by solving the Irish Question usually lacked something in the qualities of insight, imagination, and anticipation. They are best described as examples of strategic retreat and political expediency. The operating principle was to do what had to be done for England rather than what should be done for Ireland. Of course the efforts of Peel and Gladstone were in many ways exceptions to this generalization.

Over a long period of time parliamentary legislation finally satisfied the basic religious, economic, and social needs of the Irish masses. Nationalism, however, is the most powerful and persistent of modern ideologies, and it assumes an existence independent of and more important than the grievances that create and nourish it. By the late nineteenth century Britain encountered an enthusiastic and disciplined Irish nationalism unwilling to accept any alternative short of an Irish Parliament. When Conservative politicians and British opinion refused concessions to this demand, frustrated Irish nationalism became more adamant and raised the price for a settlement between the two countries. The consequences were the violence of the 1916–1922 period, a divided Ireland, and a slowly dying Irish animosity toward Britain.

While it is of value to use Ireland as an example and a preview of twentieth century tensions between the developed and underdeveloped areas of the world, this approach needs qualification. Ireland is a European, Christian nation with deep roots in Western Civilization. She is geographically close to Britain—the Irish Sea is not very wide, and in the period 1800–1922, Ireland was part of Britain, not a colony. Since Irish Catholics were a minority group in Protestant Britain, it is also valid and important to examine the Irish Question as a minority problem. In many ways Britain's Irish Question is the equivalent of the Negro Question in the United States.

In 1800 Ireland was a country with little industry and an agricultural economy not much advanced beyond the manorial system of medieval Europe. The vast majority of Irishmen were Catholic tenant farmers lacking education or economic skills. For Britain the challenge of the Irish Question was to assimilate the Catholic agrarian population and the Irish residing in the industrial cities of Britain into her economy and value system. The challenge presented a difficult but not impossible task. Britain was the most prosperous country in the world with a dynamic and varied economy. Ireland could provide food for an increasingly industrial Britain, and the surplus Irish population was a valuable manpower reserve for an industrial economy. British institutions were certainly practical and pragmatic enough to apply to the Irish people. The work capacity of Irish laborers in Britain and the United States, the achievements of Irish politicians in Parliament and in American local and national government, and the skill of Irish writers prove that the Irish people were a potential resource, but Britain wasted much of this resource.

Britain failed to meet the challenge of assimilation. This failure had many causes: a rigidity in following and applying economic theories, the conflicts of British party politics, and the no-Popery roots of British nativism. People in Britain found it difficult to accept the Irish as equal citizens. The Irish did not fit within the framework of the myths of British nationalism. Their religion and value system gave them an alien image, making them objects of fear and suspicion. The myths of British nationalism were influenced by a desire to exclude the Irish from British life. British nationalist opinion supported the privileged position of the Protestant Ascendancy in Ireland, fought concessions to Irish Catholic grievances, and isolated the Irish in Britain in slum ghettos as outsiders unworthy to share the benefits of the British community.

British laissez faire theory, associated with Liberalism, was applied as dogma in Ireland and delayed attempts to eliminate the roots of Irish economic distress. British Conservatives exploited no-Popery for political purposes and resisted reform in Ireland because such reforms might establish precedents endangering aristocratic privilege in Britain.

Reacting to the harshness of laissez faire, the indifference of British politicians to Irish distress, the machinations of British party politics, and no-Popery fanaticism, Irishmen created their own form of nationalism. The ideological premises of Irish nationalism deepened the cultural chasm separating Ireland and Britain, intensified Irish exclusiveness, and increased the problems of assimilation and mutual understanding.

Ireland was Britain's failure, perhaps her greatest, but the results of the Union were not entirely negative for either Britain or Ireland. In attempting to solve the Irish Question British politicians used Ireland as an experiment in legislation that helped undermine laissez faire dogmatism and prepare a favorable climate for the welfare state. The democratic goals of Irish agitation and the techniques of Irish agitators inspired reform movements in Britain and contributed to the eventual victory of democracy. Irish parliamentary tactics and organization did much to shape the character of the modern party system in Britain. And Britain's mistakes in Ireland taught her lessons in patience which she applied to imperial problems in the twentieth century, and probably made Englishmen more tolerant toward other peoples and cultures.

When Britain finally evacuated Ireland, she left behind many traditions and institutions. English is the language used by most Irish writers, and English is the language used by the Irish people. The Irish legal and educational systems still reflect British traditions and influences. Ireland is a parliamentary democracy and still cherishes, in theory if not always in fact, the British Liberal tradition of free thought and free speech.

Irish nationalism established pride, purpose, and dignity in the Irish population, forced reform from the British Parliament, produced talented and colorful leaders who influenced both Irish and British politics, and finally achieved a significant measure of independence for Ireland. Nationalism, however, is at its core a narrow and intolerant ideology. The nationalism of O'Connell and Young Ireland was associated with the Liberal tradition, and throughout the nineteenth and early twentieth centuries most Irish political and literary nationalists retained liberal values. Nevertheless, it is in the nature of nationalism to subordinate individual freedom to group loyalty, art to politics, and reason to fanaticism.

Delay in the achievement of Home Rule strengthened extremist elements, and as Irish nationalism moved into the twentieth century they emerged to challenge the Liberal tradition. Sinn Fein attacked the independence of the artist, and its fanaticism, evident in 1916, pushed Ireland into a fratricidal civil war following the Treaty. After 1922 Irish nationalism, short on constructive economic and social ideas, hindered the progress of the country, and narrow nationalist politics obstructed the continued excellence of Irish literature.

The prosperous, progressive, culturally active little country that was supposed to come into existence after Britain withdrew has not yet materialized. Political independence did not eliminate slums or increase the productivity of Irish agriculture. Social reform in Ireland lags behind achievements in most of Western Europe, emigration continues to drain real and potential talent, and the Irish people, to say the least, are not enthusiastic about culture. To idealists, all of this seems disappointing after the expectations of O'Connell, Young Ireland, the Fenians, Home Rulers, Sinn Fein, and the artists of the literary revival. Nationalism achieved self-government, but it has obstructed the energy, imagination, and ambition of the Irish people.

Exploiting nationalist sentiment among the voters, Irish politicians, while campaigning for office, concentrate attention on past British wrongs, Partition, or the issues of the civil war. These patriotic exercises have been at the expense of realistic evaluations of economic needs and programs for social reform. Irish businessmen have insisted on protection against foreign competition. Protection has often led Ireland in wrong economic directions by encouraging the multiplication of inefficient industries producing shoddy consumer goods. Irish education needs many improvements: more and better schools, a richer curriculum, and increased vocational training in the areas of technology and agriculture. But Gaelic Leaguers, by insisting on compulsory Irish, a language not used by the people, have added to the obstacles hindering educational progress.

The Catholic Church, the most powerful institution in Ireland, remains a peasant, unsophisticated church, not much influenced by the progressive tendencies evident in the Catholicism practiced in most of the Western world. Bishops and priests resent what they consider to be the pretensions of lay intellectualism and leadership. They have teamed up with the politicians to support censorship, one technique in a grand strategy to isolate "holy Ireland" from the pagan spirit of the modern world. Censorship was supposed to protect the moral fiber of Irish life from alien, secular, immoral, and subversive ideas. Isolation, if it could work, might for a time shelter a country from the unrest troubling the rest of the world, but it has the unfortunate effect of cutting her people off from the mainstreams of culture. Those intellectuals and writers who protest against chauvinism, the restrictions of the Irish way of life, and the narrowness of Irish Catholicism offend the thin skinned Irish community. They have been criticized as unpatriotic or irreligious and encouraged to practice their skills and art in other countries.

Recent events in other emerging nations have emphasized the wide gulf that exists between the dreams of revolutionaries and the realities of post-revolutionary politics. The actualities of contemporary Ireland fall short of the expectations of the heroes of Irish nationalism, but perhaps that is an impractical standard by which to judge the success of a relatively new nation. Without many natural resources or vocationally trained people, burdened by the psychological blocks that are produced by an unfortunate historical experience, and lacking sophisticated political leadership, Ireland since 1922 has been a relatively stable nation and even a moderately progressive one.

Within the last ten years some industrial development has come to Ireland, opening up all sorts of economic possibilities and providing an alternative to emigration. Ireland has assumed international responsibilities in the work of the United Nations. Her representatives to that organization have been outstanding in talent. They believe that the historical experience of their country puts them in an excellent position to express the attitudes and aspirations of emerging nations. Censorship, though still on the books, has been relaxed as the effort to isolate Ireland has been defeated by modern communication and transportation and the tastes of a more prosperous and sophisticated generation of Irishmen. Perhaps the Catholic Church in Ireland will catch the spirit of John XXIII, and some observers say that there are signs that she might.

In the fifty years since 1916 Ireland seems to have developed confidence and maturity, and half a century is not a long time in the history of a nation. It is possible that a more sophisticated Ireland and a more tolerant Britain will achieve a substantial measure of cooperation and understanding, even unity, in the Common Market, perhaps in a united Western Europe, certainly in a common allegiance to the values of Western Civilization.

Recommended Reading

GENERAL WORKS

J. C. Beckett, *The Making of Modern Ireland, 1603-1923* (New York: Knopf, 1966).

Thomas W. Freeman, *Ireland: A General and Regional Geography,* 2nd ed. (London: Methuen, 1960).

Nicholas Mansergh, *The Irish Question, 1840-1920,* rev. ed. (Toronto: University of Toronto Press, 1966).

R. B. McDowell, *The Irish Administration, 1801-1914* (Toronto: University of Toronto Press, 1964).

Patrick S. O'Hegarty, *A History of Ireland Under the Union, 1801 to 1922* (London: Methuen, 1952).

Eric Strauss, *Irish Nationalism and British Democracy* (New York: Columbia University Press, 1951).

CATHOLIC EMANCIPATION, 1800-1829

POLITICAL BACKGROUND

G. C. Bolton, *The Passing of the Irish Act of Union* (London: Oxford University Press, 1966).

R. B. McDowell, *Public Opinion and Government Policy in Ireland, 1801-1846* (New York: Hillary, 1952).

SOCIAL AND ECONOMIC BACKGROUND

Kenneth H. Connell, *The Population of Ireland, 1750-1845* (London: Oxford University Press, 1950).

Thomas W. Freeman, *Pre-Famine Ireland: A Study in Historical Geography* (Manchester: Manchester University Press, 1957).

THE POSITION OF THE CATHOLICS BEFORE EMANCIPATION

Robert E. Burns, "The Irish Penal Code and Some of its Historians," *Review of Politics*, XXI (January, 1959), 276-99.

————, "The Irish Popery Laws: A Study of Eighteenth Century Legislation and Behavior," *Review of Politics*, XXIV (October, 1962), 485-508.

Maurice R. O'Connell, *Irish Politics and Social Conflict in the Age of the American Revolution* (Philadelphia: University of Pennsylvania Press, 1965).

Maureen Wall, *The Penal Laws, 1691-1760*, Irish History Series, No. 1 (Dundalk: Dundalgan Press Ltd., for the Dublin Historical Association, 1961).

————, "The Rise of a Catholic Middle Class in Eighteenth Century Ireland," *Irish Historical Studies*, XI (September, 1958), 91-115.

DANIEL O'CONNELL

Robert Dunlop, *Daniel O'Connell and the Revival of National Life in Ireland* (New York: Putnam, 1900).

Denis Gwynn, *Daniel O'Connell: The Irish Liberator* (Cork: Cork University Press, 1947).

William Edward Hartpole Lecky, "Daniel O'Connell," *The Leaders of Public Opinion in Ireland* (London: Longmans, Greene, 1871, 1883, 1903).

Sean O'Faolain, *King of Beggars* (New York: Viking Press, 1938).

Michael Tierney (ed.), *Daniel O'Connell* (Dublin: Browne and Nolan, 1949).

(The O'Faolain and Lecky portraits are probably the best biographical studies of O'Connell.)

THE CATHOLIC ASSOCIATION AND THE AGITATION
FOR CATHOLIC EMANCIPATION

James A. Reynolds, *The Catholic Emancipation Crisis in Ireland, 1823-1829* (New Haven: Yale University Press, 1954).

CATHOLIC EMANCIPATION AND BRITISH POLITICS

Norman Gash, *Mr. Secretary Peel* (Cambridge, Mass.: Harvard University Press, 1961).

G. I. T. Machin, *The Catholic Question in English Politics, 1820-1830* (London: Oxford University Press, 1964).

REPEAL, 1829-1845

O'CONNELL, IRISH NATIONALISTS, AND THE BRITISH PARLIAMENT

Thomas N. Brown, "Nationalism and the Irish Peasant," *Review of Politics*, XV (October, 1953), 403-445.

Norman Gash, *Politics in the Age of Peel* (London: Longmans, Greene, 1953).

A. H. Graham, "The Lichfield House Compact, 1835," *Irish Historical Studies*, XII (March, 1961), 209-225.

David Large, "The House of Lords and Ireland in the Age of Peel, 1832-1850," *Irish Historical Studies*, IX (September, 1955), 367-69.

Angus MacIntyre, *The Liberator: Daniel O'Connell and the Irish Party, 1830-1847* (London: H. Hamilton, 1965).

John H. Whyte, "Daniel O'Connell and the Repeal Party," *Irish Historical Studies*, XI (September, 1959), 297-316.

THE REPEAL AGITATION AND PEEL'S IRISH POLICY

Gilbert Cahill, "Irish Catholicism and English Toryism," *Review of Politics*, XIX (January, 1957), 62-76.

————, "The Protestant Association and the Anti-Maynooth Agitation of 1845," *Catholic Historical Review*, XLIII (October, 1957), 273-308.

George Kitson-Clark, *Peel and the Conservative Party: A Study in Party Politics, 1822-1841*, 2nd ed. (Hamden, Conn.: Archon Books, 1964).

Lawrence J. McCaffrey, *Daniel O'Connell and the Repeal Year* (Lexington: University of Kentucky Press, 1966).

Kevin Nowlan, *The Politics of Repeal* (Toronto: University of Toronto Press, 1965).

————, "The Meaning of Repeal in Church History," *Historical Studies*, IV, papers read at the Fifth Conference of Irish Historians, London, 1963.

YOUNG IRELAND AND CULTURAL NATIONALISM

Charles Gavan Duffy, *Young Ireland* (London: T. Fisher Unwin, 1896).

Thomas Flanagan, *The Irish Novelists, 1800-1850* (New York: Columbia University Press, 1959).

Benedict Kiely, *Poor Scholar: A Study of the Works and Days of William Carleton, 1794-1869* (London: Sheed and Ward, 1947).

CLERICALISM, CATHOLICISM, AND IRISH NATIONALISM

John F. Broderick, S.J., *The Holy See and the Irish Movement for the Repeal of the Union with England, 1829-1847* (Rome: Universitatis Gregorianae, 1951).

Emmet Larkin, "Church and State in Ireland in the Nineteenth Century, *Church History*, XXI (September, 1962), 294-306.

————, "The Quarrel Among the Roman Catholic Hierarchy over the National System of Education in Ireland, 1838-1841," *The Celtic*

Cross, ed. Ray B. Browne, William J. Roscelli, and Richard J. Loftus (Lafayette, Ind.: Purdue University, 1964).

John H. Whyte, "The Influence of the Catholic Clergy on Elections in Nineteenth Century Ireland," *English Historical Review*, LXXV (April, 1960), 239-259.

—————, "The Appointment of Catholic Bishops in Nineteenth Century Ireland," *Catholic Historical Review*, XLVIII (April, 1962), 12-32.

FAMINE, REVOLUTION, AND REPUBLICANISM

THE FAMINE

R. D. Collison Black, *Economic Thought and the Irish Question, 1817-1870* (Cambridge: Cambridge University Press, 1960).

R. Dudley Edwards and T. Desmond Williams (eds.), *The Great Famine: Studies in Irish History, 1845-1852* (Dublin: published for the Irish Committee for Historical Sciences by Browne and Nolan, 1956).

Cecil Woodham-Smith, *The Great Hunger, Ireland, 1845-49* (New York: Harper, 1962).

R. N. Salaman, *The History and Social Influence of the Potato* (Cambridge, Mass.: Harvard University Press, 1949).

1848

Denis Gwynn, *O'Connell, Davis, and the Colleges Bill* (Cork: Cork University Press, 1948).

—————, *Young Ireland and 1848* (Cork: Cork University Press, 1949).

Thomas P. O'Neill, "The Economic and Political Ideas of James Fintan Lalor," *Irish Ecclesiastical Record*, LXXIV (November, 1950), 398-409.

THE INDEPENDENT IRISH PARTY

John H. Whyte, *The Independent Irish Party, 1850-1859* (London: Oxford University Press, 1958).

FENIANISM, EMIGRATION, AND IRISH NATIONALISM
IN BRITAIN AND AMERICA

Thomas N. Brown, "The Origins and Character of Irish American Nationalism," *Review of Politics*, XVIII (July, 1956), 327-58. (Also helpful was Brown's yet unpublished paper, "Parnell and the American Irish," which was read at the American Historical Association meeting in Philadelphia, 1963).

—————, *Irish American Nationalism* (Philadelphia: Lippincott, 1966).

—————, "Nationalism and the Irish Peasant, 1800-1848," *Review of Politics*, XV (October, 1953), 403-45.

William D'Arcy, *The Fenian Movement in the United States, 1858-1886* (Washington: Catholic University of America, 1947).

Oscar Handlin, *Boston's Immigrants* (Cambridge, Mass.: Harvard University Press, 1959).

John Archer Jackson, *The Irish in Britain* (Cleveland: Western Reserve University Press, 1963).

William O'Brien and Desmond Ryan (eds.), *Devoy's Post-Bag, 1871-1928*, introduction by Patrick S. O'Hegarty, 2 vols, (Dublin: Fallon, 1948, 1953).

Arnold Schrier, *Ireland and the American Emigration 1850-1900* (Minneapolis: University of Minnesota Press, 1958).

William V. Shannon, *The American Irish* (New York: Macmillan, 1963).

Carl Wittke, *The Irish in America* (Baton Rouge: Louisiana State University Press, 1956).

GLADSTONE'S IRISH POLICY

J. L. Hammond, *Gladstone and the Irish Nation*, 2nd ed. (Hamden, Conn.: Shoe String Press, 1964).

THE NATIONAL ASSOCIATION

E. R. Norman, *The Catholic Church and Ireland in the Age of Rebellion, 1859-1873* (Ithaca, N.Y.: Cornell University Press, 1965). (Norman has some excellent material on the Catholic Church and Fenianism).

HOME RULE, 1870-1880

POLITICAL BACKGROUND

Terence deVere White, *The Road of Excess: A Biography of Isaac Butt* (Dublin: Browne and Nolan, 1946).

H. J. Hanham, *Elections and Party Management: Politics in the Time of Disraeli and Gladstone* (New York: Humanities Press, 1959).

Lawrence J. McCaffrey, *Irish Federalism in the 1870's: A Study in Conservative Nationalism* (Philadelphia: American Philosophical Society, 1962).

David Thornley, *Isaac Butt and Home Rule* (London: Ambassador Press, 1964).

THE NEW DEPARTURE

T. W. Moody, "The New Departure in Irish Politics, 1878-79," *Essays in British and Irish History in Honour of James Eadie Todd* (London: Muller, 1949).

Norman Palmer, *The Irish Land League Crisis* (New Haven: Yale University Press, 1940).

John Pomfret, *The Struggle for Land in Ireland* (Princeton: Princeton University Press, 1930).
(The interpretation of the New Departure in my book is borrowed from an unpublished essay by Thomas N. Brown, "The New Departure, 1879-1880," which was read before the Irish Historical Society, Dublin, March, 1958).

HOME RULE, 1880-1906

PARNELL AND THE IRISH PARTY

W. L. Arnstein, "Parnell and the Bradlaugh Case," *Irish Historical Studies*, XIII (March, 1963), 212-35.
John A. Glaser, "Parnell's Fall and the Nonconformist Conscience," *Irish Historical Studies*, XII (September, 1960), 119-38.
Emmet Larkin, "The Roman Catholic Hierarchy and the Fall of Parnell," *Victorian Studies*, IV (June, 1961), 315-36.
————, "Mounting the Counter-Attack: The Roman Catholic Hierarchy and the Destruction of Parnellism," Review of Politics, XXV (April, 1963), 157-82.
F. S. L. Lyons, *The Irish Parliamentary Party, 1890-1910* (London: Faber and Faber, 1951).
————, *The Fall of Parnell, 1890-1891* (Toronto: University of Toronto Press, 1960).
H. W. McCready, "Home Rule and the Liberal Party, 1880-1901," *Irish Historical Studies*, XIII (September, 1963), 316-48.
Conor Cruise O'Brien, *Parnell and His Party, 1880-1890* (London: Oxford University Press, 1957).

THE IRISH QUESTION AND BRITISH POLITICS AND INSTITUTIONS

Lewis P. Curtis, Jr., *Coercion and Conciliation in Ireland, 1880-1892: A Study in Conservative Unionism* (Princeton: Princeton University Press, 1963).
Helen Merrell Lynd, *England in the 1880's: Toward a Social Basis for Freedom* (London: Oxford University Press, 1945).

THE CRISIS OF IRISH NATIONALISM, 1906-1914

POLITICAL BACKGROUND

Mary Bromage, *Churchill and Ireland* (South Bend, Ind.: Notre Dame University Press, 1965).
George Dangerfield, *The Strange Death of Liberal England* (New York: Putnam, 1935).
Sir James Fergusson, *The Curragh Incident* (London: Faber and Faber, 1964).

Denis Gwynn, *The Life of John Redmond* (London: Harrap, 1932).
Roy Jenkins, *Asquith* (London: Collins, 1965).
Conor Cruise O'Brien (ed.), *The Shaping of Modern Ireland* (Toronto: University of Toronto Press, 1960).
A. P. Ryan, *Mutiny at the Curragh* (London: St. Martins, 1956).

THE ULSTER QUESTION

M. W. Heslinga, *The Irish Border as a Culture Divide* (New York: Humanities Press, 1962).
T. W. Moody and J. C. Beckett (eds.), *Ulster Since 1800: A Political and Economic Survey* (London: published by the British Broadcasting Co., 1955).
————— (eds.), *Ulster Since 1800: A Social Survey* (London: published by the British Broadcasting Co., 1957).
D. C. Savage, "The Origins of the Ulster Unionist Party, 1885-1886," *Irish Historical Studies*, XII (March, 1961), 185-208.
Hereward Senior, *Orangeism in Ireland and Britain, 1795-1836* (New York: Hillary, 1966).

THE RISE OF LABOR

J. Dunsmore Clarkson, *Labour and Nationalism in Ireland* (New York: Columbia University Press, 1925).
Emmet Larkin, *James Larkin, Irish Labour Leader, 1876-1947* (Cambridge, Mass.: M.I.T. Press, 1965).

THE RESURGENCE OF CULTURAL NATIONALISM

Herbert Howarth, *The Irish Writers: Literature and Nationalism, 1880-1940* (New York: Hill and Wang, 1958).
Richard J. Loftus, *Nationalism in Modern Anglo-Irish Poetry* (Madison: University of Wisconsin Press, 1964). The Loftus book also has great value as a source for the next chapter.

THE ROSE TREE, 1914-1922

Richard Bennett, *The Black and Tans* (Boston: Hougton-Mifflin, 1959).
Mary C. Bromage, *DeValera and the March of a Nation* (London: Hutchinson, 1956).
Edgar Holt, *Protest in Arms: The Irish Troubles, 1916-1923* (London, McClelland, 1960). Holt's book is exceptionally readable, fair, and accurate.
Dorothy Macardle, *The Irish Republic* (London: Farrar, Straus, 1965).
Frank Pakenham, *Peace by Ordeal* (Toronto: Nelson, 1935).
Desmond Williams (ed), *The Irish Struggle, 1916-1926* (Toronto: University of Toronto Press, 1966).

Since this is a study of the Irish Question and its influence on the evolution of Irish Nationalism and on British politics and institutions and not a comprehensive history of Ireland 1800-1922, I have not attempted a complete bibliography. For a definitive bibliography of recent material see Helen F. Mulvey, "Modern Irish History Since 1940: A Bibliographical Survey (1600-1922)," *The Historian,* XXVII (August, 1965), 516-59.

Index